Sylvanus Stall

What a young husband ought to know

Sylvanus Stall

What a young husband ought to know

ISBN/EAN: 9783741155383

Manufactured in Europe, USA, Canada, Australia, Japa

Cover: Foto ©Andreas Hilbeck / pixelio.de

Manufactured and distributed by brebook publishing software
(www.brebook.com)

Sylvanus Stall

What a young husband ought to know

CHARLES M. SHELDON, D.D.

Author of "In His Steps," "Crucifixion of Philip Strong,"
"My Brother's Keeper," etc., etc.,
Topeka, Kans.

"I take pleasure in adding my word of commendation for the spirit and purpose of your book, 'What a Young Husband Ought to Know,' which I have received and read. I believe the book will do great good, and I hope its message may be used for the bettering of the homes of the world."

REV. F. B. MEYER, B.A.

Minister of Christ Church, Westminster, London, Author of "Israel, A Prince with God," "Elijah; Tried by Fire," "The Bells of Is," etc., etc.

"The questions which are dealt with in the 'Self and Sex Series' of books are always being asked, and if the answer is not forthcoming from pure and wise lips it will be obtained through vicious and empirical channels. I therefore greatly commend this series of manuals, which are written lucidly and purely, and will afford the necessary information without pandering to unholy and sensual passion. There has been, in my judgment, too much reticence on the whole of this subject, and nameless sins have originated in ignorance or in the directions given to young life by vicious men. I should like to see a wide and judicious distribution of this literature among Christian circles."

HON. S. M. JONES.
Mayor of Toledo, Ohio.

"I have taken the time out of a very hurried week to look over your book, 'What a Young Husband Ought to Know,' and it seems to me that it is a work that has been prepared with great care and discrimination. I have often thought that this work is one that some heart inspired by love of humanity should undertake. I am glad to say that my study of it indicates that you have been led by a pure love for your kind to write one of the most helpful and valuable books that it has been my privilege to see in many days."

What Eminent People in America Say

EDWARD BOK.

Editor of the "Ladies' Home Journal."

"You have accomplished in doing, in your little book, 'What a Young Husband Ought to Know,' exactly what you have set out to do, it seems to me, and I know of no book of its kind which exhales to the same degree, and so unerringly, the candid, pure and exalted purpose of the writer. It is an honest little book, and every young married man who reads it cannot fail to be helped by it, and helped materially. There are books, three times the size, which do not begin to have one-third of the common sense in them that your little book has."

MRS. HELEN CAMPBELL.

Dean of the Department of Household Economics, Kansas State Agricultural College; author of "Prisoners of Poverty," "Some Passages in the Life of Dr. Martha Scarborough," etc., etc.

"It meets the strongest need for the mass of young men, who have failed most of them, to receive the training outlined in the books for boys—who are ignorant utterly as to just their own degree of responsibility, and who will find in your careful statement of the problem as a whole, not only invaluable direction, but a guarantee of healthier and happier life for both husband and wife."

WHAT EMINENT PEOPLE IN AMERICA SAY.

MRS. MAY WRIGHT SEWALL.

President of the Girls' Classical School; President of the International Council of Women.

"I feel sure that the book which you have had the privilege to write must do every young man good who reads it. To inculcate in society this sound view that knowledge upon these subjects is not only compatible with delicacy, but requisite to it, is one of the most important contemporary duties of teachers, whether in the pulpit, on the rostrum, in the sanctum. or in the class-room."

HERRICK JOHNSON, D.D., LL.D.

Professor in McCormick Theological Seminary, Chicago. Author of "Plain Talks about the Theatre," "Revivals, Their Place and Power," "Christianity's Challenge," etc.

"I have just laid down your book, 'What a Young Husband Ought to Know,' after a very interested perusal of it. The rare discrimination and delicate sense displayed in the handling of your theme are especially commendable. To say a bold courageous thing on a confessedly delicate subject, without any offence to true modesty, is a fine achievement. All manhood and womanhood ought to thank you."

What Eminent People in America Say.

BISHOP JOHN H. VINCENT, D.D., LL.D.

Chancellor of the Chautauqua Literary and Scientific Circle; Author of "Sunday School Institutes and Normal Classes," "The Church School and Its Officers," etc.

' In a straightforward, clean, kind, clear and convincing way you discuss the ' Young Husband' question. A copy ought to go with every marriage certificate. The book is timely and full of wisdom."

FRANCIS E. CLARKE, D D.

Founder of the Young People's Society of Christian Endeavor, and President of the United Society.

"I regard Dr. Stall's latest book as equal to the others in its delicate but plain-spoken chapters concerning the facts the men to whom it is addressed ought to know. I hope it will have a wide circulation."

JOSIAH STRONG, D.D.

President of the League for Social Service; Author of "Our Country," "New Era," "The Twentieth Century City," etc.

"'What a Young Husband Ought to Know,' like the earlier books of the series, is judicious in its selection of topics and wise in its treatment of them. Your admirable work will enable many young husbands to learn what they ought to know without paying the high tuition fee exacted in the school of experience."

MRS. FRANCES SHELDON BOLTON.

Editor of "Mothers' Journal;" Author of "Baby" and Other Books.

"What a vast amount of suffering and wretchedness would be prevented, and how many happy homes could be saved, if all young men before they are married would read and profit by Dr. Sylvanus Stall's book, entitled 'What a Young Husband Ought to Know.'"

EMILY S. BOUTON.

Author of " Health and Beauty," " Social Etiquette," "House and Domestic Decorations," " Life's Gateways and How to Win Real Success," etc.

"It is much to find a writer who may touch upon these subjects with a strong, firm, true, and yet delicate pen; and you are doing good service to humanity by such work. I am indeed glad to know that your former works have been so highly commended, and where such commendation will do great good."

REV. NEWELL DWIGHT HILLIS.

Pastor of Plymouth Church, Brooklyn, N. Y., and author of "The Investment of Influence," "A Man's Value to Society," etc.

"I have read your book with care and interest. It is a wholesome and helpful contribution to a most difficult subject, and its reading will help to make the American home happier and more safely guarded."

HOWARD A. KELLY, M.D.

Professor of Gynecology and Obstetrics Johns Hopkins University, Baltimore, Md.

"The book 'What a Young Husband Ought to Know' can be heartily recommended. It handles in a plain but delicate and reverential manner subjects that should be thoroughly understood by every adult man, but which often are first learned by him through bitter experience. If the knowledge contained in it were more generally diffused, many sad duties left for the physician would become unnecessary."

LEMUEL BOLTON BANGS, M.D.

Professor Genito-Urinary Surgery in the N. Y. Post-Graduate Medical School; Consulting Surgeon to St. Luke's Hospital and to the Methodist Episcopal Hospital, Brooklyn: Surgeon to the City Hospital, N. Y.

"I have recommended it to a good many *old* as well as 'young' husbands, and am satisfied of its usefulness to them. I shall continue to commend it, and also the other books of the series."

EUGENE H. PORTER, M A., M.D.

Professor Materia Medica, New York Homœopathic Medical College ; Professor Diseases of Stomach and Liver, Metropolitan Post-Graduate School ; Author of numerous standard medical works ; Editor of North American Journal of Homœopathy.

"Your new book, 'What a Young Husband Ought to Know,' should be in the hands of every young man who contemplates marriage. The work, while thoroughly refined in style and treatment, is vigorous and direct in its teaching and application of essential truths. Purity, happiness and health will be with those who heed its teachings. It is a sound and practical volume, and deserves a wide circulation."

H J. BOLDT, M.D.

Professor of Gynæcology, New York Post Graduate Medical School and Hospital ; Gynæcologist to St. Mark's Hospital ; Gynæcologist to the German Poliklinik.

"There is nothing in the book which every man entering upon such new duty in life should not know. I personally feel that its possession, and *following* it in practice by young husbands, would be conducive to a purer life and more happiness. I shall most cheerfully commend it whenever an opportunity presents itself."

OLIVER EDWARD JANNEY, M.D.

The Southern Homœopathic Medical College, Baltimore, Md.

"If it could be placed in the hands of prospective husbands a vast amount of unhappiness and disease would be avoided, and the well-being of the race advanced. It is not wickedness, but ignorance that wrecks lives on the threshold of marriage, and this book *teaches*."

PAUL F. MUNDÈ, M.D., LL.D.

Professor of Gynæcology at the New York Polyclinic and at Dartmouth College; Gynæcologist to Mount Sinai Hospital.

"I have looked through your book, entitled, 'What a Young Husband Ought to Know,' and am impelled by its contents and the careful and delicate manner in which you endeavor to communicate to a man about to enter the married state, 'what EVERY young husband ought to know,' if he would ensure his marital happiness and save his wife as much as possible from the many afflictions unfortunately not always separable from that state. I am impelled, I repeat, to depart from my custom of refusing to endorse semi-medical publications intended for the lay-reader. Your previous work on 'What a Young Man Ought to Know,' has once before induced me to commit the same departure, and I feel that I am but adding my humble share toward the good work which I think you are conscientiously endeavoring to perform, in repeating substantially the commendation of the former book as applied to the present."

Pure Books on Avoided Subjects

Books for Men

By *Sylvanus Stall, D. D.*

"What a Young Boy Ought to Know."
"What a Young Man Ought to Know."
"What a Young Husband Ought to Know."
"What a Man of 45 Ought to Know."

Books for Women

By *Mrs. Mary Wood-Allen, M. D.,*
And *Mrs. Emma F. A. Drake, M. D.*

"What a Young Girl Ought to Know."
"What a Young Woman Ought to Know."
"What a Young Wife Ought to Know."
"What a Woman of 45 Ought to Know."

PRICE AND BINDING

The books are issued in uniform size and but one style of binding, and sell in America at $1, in Great Britian at 4s., net, per copy, post free, whether sold singly or in sets.

PUBLISHED BY

IN THE UNITED STATES

THE VIR PUBLISHING COMPANY
2237 Land Title Building   Philadelphia

IN ENGLAND

THE VIR PUBLISHING COMPANY
7 Imperial Arcade, Ludgate Circus, London, E.C.

IN CANADA

WILLIAM BRIGGS
29-33 Richmond Street West   Toronto, Ontario

SYLVANUS STALL, D.D.

Price $1.00 net
4s. net

PURITY AND TRUTH

WHAT A YOUNG HUSBAND OUGHT TO KNOW

BY

SYLVANUS STALL, D. D.

Author of "What a Young Boy Ought to Know," "What a Young Man Ought to Know," "What a Man of 45 Ought to Know," "Methods of Church Work," "Five-Minute Object Sermons to Children," "Talks to the King's Children," "Faces Toward the Light," etc.

"*The Glory of Young Men is Their Strength.*"

Philadelphia, Pa.: 2237 Land Title Building.

THE VIR PUBLISHING COMPANY

London:
7, Imperial Arcade,
Ludgate Circus, E. C.

Toronto:
Wm. Briggs,
33 Richmond St, West.

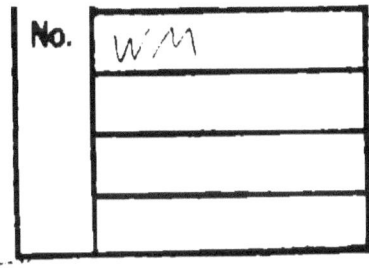

Copyright, 1897, by SYLVANUS STALL

Entered at Stationers' Hall, London, England

Protected by International copyright in Great Britain and all her colonies, and, under the provisions of the Berne Convention, in Belgium, France, Germany, Italy, Spain, Switzerland, Tunis, Hayti, Luxembourg, Monaco, Montenegro, and Norway

All rights reserved

[PRINTED IN THE UNITED STATES]

Dedicated

TO

THE SANCTITY OF HOME, THE PURITY AND BLESSING
OF THE HUSBAND AND WIFE, AND THE WELL-
BEING OF THEIR OFFSPRING

CONTENTS.

PART I.

CONCERNING HIMSELF.

CHAPTER I.

THE RELATION OF MARRIAGE.

PAGE

The new relation full of new meaning.—Lifted into a higher realm.—Love transforms the nature.—Marriage the estate of man's highest happiness.—The awakening of reproductive life in field and forest.—These powers may be held in abeyance.—They also have their proper exercise.—Reason to rule over passion.—The need of a strong emotional nature in men and in women.—Sexual nature should not be immolated.—Vice and lust cannot bring happiness.—The sensual usurper must be deposed and love enthroned.—This our effort and our justification, ...   25

CHAPTER II.

DIFFERENCES OF SEX.

Each sex superior in its sphere.—Two parts of a complete unit.—Differences between men and women.—Physically.—Intellectually.—These differences complemental.—The more nervous sensibilities of woman.—The earliest manifestation of sex characteristics.—All life from an egg.—The human egg, size, etc.—The ovum always passive.—The spermatozoön, or sperm, always active.—Their remarkable vitality.—The quicker pulse of male children at birth.—

Greater activity of boys.—While more male children are born, a larger per cent. die in infancy.—Women endure more and live longer.—Woman's more passive nature recognized by the civil law, ... 31

CHAPTER III.

DIFFERENCES OF SEX.

(Continued.)

Women keep life stable.—Men keep it from stagnation.—Influence of each a corrective upon the other.—The law of mental and physical resemblance of elderly married persons.—Why woman possesses the stronger moral nature.—How husband and children are benefited.—The savage tribes manifest the dominant male characteristics.—Civilized nations take upon them the best characteristics of the feminine type.—The best characteristics of each sex finds modified expression in the other.—The beneficial effects which God secures by the union of an active with a passive sexual nature in marriage.—The well-being of both bettered.—Mutual intelligence begets harmony, while ignorance produces discord and misery.—The reproductive organs differentiated in man and in woman.—The same organs modified, differently placed, and assigned a different office, . . 41

CHAPTER IV.

ESSENTIALS IN HUSBAND AND HOME.

Requisites in a good husband.—Woman's love of home and its adornments.—Keeping up the courtship.—The home, the club, and the loafing-place.—An instance in point.—The right of the wife to share the husband's recreations, diversions and pleasures.—The wife's greater need of relaxation and diversion.—Dr. Farrar's picture of a considerate husband,—Woman's love of being wooed.—Not marriage, but the parties to it, often a failure.—Degraded views concerning women often held.—Domineering wives and husbands.—The Zuni Indians.—The Scriptural teaching.—Industry essential to happiness in the home.—The claims of religion to be recognized.—The conditions of the wicked and godly contrasted.—The promise of the life that now is, as well as that which is to come, ... 53

CHAPTER V.

THE PHYSICAL COST OF PROCREATION.

Boxing the compass, or proving the principles.—Prevalent ignorance on subjects relating to sex.—Lessons taught by the reproduction of vegetable life.—The green scum of the pond.—Reproduction costs life.—Death as the result of reproduction among fishes. — Reproduction among insects.—The drone and the queen bee.—With the birds, death as the result of reproduction disappears.—With animals, the ovum and sperm are reduced to microscopic proportions.—The inclination to beget, a premonition of decay and death.—Procreation costs vital force. — Reproductive inclination periodic among the lower animals.—More continuous in man.—Benefits of restraint.—Strict continence often an imperative duty.—Instances named, ... 74

CHAPTER VI.

MARITAL MODERATION.

Twofold nature of love.—Rooted in the physical, flowers in the spiritual.—Lust often miscalled love.—Three theories concerning the marital relation.—Unrestrained indulgence for men.—For procreation only.—As an expression of affection and for mutual endearment.—The perpetuity of the race and the highest good of the individual consistent.—What is marital moderation?—Difficulty in defining.—The reproductive sense, like hunger, to be brought under the dominion of intelligence and refinement.—The worm and the wild animals contrasted with man in the satisfying of hunger.—Jeremy Taylor's rule.—Strong words from Mrs. E. B. Duffey.—Marital moderation vs. conjugal debauchery.—Limits set by some physicians.—No one rule equally applicable in all cases.—Physical conditions of both husband and wife to be considered.—Degrading effects of sexual excess.—The wishes of the wife always to be respected.—Stimulating food, books, pictures, etc.—Importance of single beds and separate apartments.—Opinions of others quoted.—Physical culture as a corrective.—Manly mastery worth all it costs.—The struggle not endless, ... 85

CHAPTER VII.
DEFECTS AND DEFICIENCIES.

Apprehensions awakened.—Foolish and injurious expedients resorted to.—Actual impotence not frequent.—Consult only intelligent and conscientious physicians.—How to remove the apprehension.—Defects and deficiencies even less prevalent among females than among males.—Importance of proper treatment of the bride.—Rareness of deformity and abnormal conditions.—Weakness and diseased condition of the womb frequent among women.—No woman with serious womb trouble should marry.—How actual conditions can be accurately and properly determined, ... 103

CHAPTER VIII.
PURITY AND FIDELITY.

Happiness dependent upon plain everyday principles.—The defilement of the breath.—Effects on wife of the use of tobacco by the husband.—Effects upon physical and intellectual inheritance of offspring—Effects of the use of liquor upon progeny.—The duty of fidelity.—One standard for both husband and wife.—The physical risks of impurity.—The sufferings of innocent and unsuspecting wives.—An impressive illustration.—Terrible effects suffered by wives as result of gonorrhœa in husbands.—Unmistakable testimony of eminent physicians.—Not only physical effects upon wife, but moral effects upon self and children, . 110

PART II.

CONCERNING HIS WIFE.

CHAPTER IX.

THE BRIDE.

Importance of knowledge contained in preceding volume.—Woman possessed of less sexual inclinations than man.—Threefold classification.—Those largely devoid of sexual feeling.—This condition accounted for.—The large class to whom the pleasure is normal.—The third class consists of those in whom sexuality is a ruling passion.—Misfortune of such a condition in a wife.—Among animals the female determines the time of mating.—No rapes among animals.—The subjugation of the wife.—Her right over her own body.—The changes which come to the reproductive natures of men and women at middle life.—Noticeable effect of the new relation upon young married people.—The cause and cure of excessive sensual tendencies, ... 123

CHAPTER X.

THE CARE OF THE BRIDE.

Few young husbands intelligent guardians of their brides.—Many brides totally ignorant of everything relating to sex.—Depleted physical condition of most brides.—Ignorant brides and inconsiderate husbands.—Estrangement often begins with marriage.—The Grecian custom a good one.—An instance where passion and impatience resulted in a permanent separation.—Plain words by Dr. Guernsey.—Mrs. Duffey's warnings to rapacious young husbands.—Serious physical effects.—Dr. Napheys on the precipitancy of young husbands.—Physical inconvenience and discomfort of young brides.—What may be regarded as sufficient evidence of virginity.—Medical authorities quoted.—Idiots and imbeciles begotten as result of liquor used on wedding occasions.—Wedding joy "too good to last."—The wave cannot remain at its crest.—Have a home.—Dangers of hotel and boarding-house life.—Danger from debt.—Industry, happiness and health.—How to have joy abide to the end, ... 132

CHAPTER XI.

THE YOUNG WIFE AND MOTHERHOOD.

Manifold duties of the wife.—The great army of martyred wives and mothers.—Need of consideration on the part of husbands.—Parenthood the great purpose of marriage.—The great wrong of purposed and persistent evasion of parenthood.—It places lust upon the throne of love.—Such evasions always punished by nature.—Queen Victoria as a model mother.—Motherhood may not properly be forced upon an unwilling wife.—How to effect the necessary change of mind.—Why many wives are unwilling to become mothers.—How children mold the characters of husband and wife.—Children golden links to bind husband and wife more closely.—They are buffers to break the jars of family life.—They become their parents' benefactors.—Desire for children natural and commendable. — Barrenness.—Causes of, ... 146

CHAPTER XII.

QUESTIONS CONCERNING OFFSPRING.

Natural for parents to desire offspring.—The prevalent unnatural desire to evade parenthood. —The crime of destroying unborn human life. —The law pronounces the crime murder.—The question of quickening. — Authorities quoted.—How the health and lives of mothers are sacrificed by abortion.—Character of "unwanted" children.—The desire to murder transmitted from mother to child.—The transmission of a predisposition to commit murder. —How the minds of young girls are prepared for child-murder.—Defective instruction and consequent ignorance.—How husbands drive wives to commit this great crime.—Awful testimony of wives.—The largest reproduction possible not intended.—Quantity as well as quality.—Culpable and criminal limitation of offspring.—Times when it is wrong to beget children.—Difficulties may be removed and fitness acquired.—How may the birth rate be rightly regulated?—What physicians say.— Unsafe, unsatisfactory and ruinous methods resorted to.—The Scriptural provision.—Benefits and dangers of "Prepared Parenthood."— Mental state at time of conjunction.—Mental and physical state of mother during gestation. —Signs of fruitful conjunction, .   162

CHAPTER XIII.

THE EXPECTANT MOTHER.

During maternity the wife should have special consideration.—Lack of intelligence often inspires fear and dread.—Discouraging and depressing remarks of some women to expectant young mothers.—How to overcome her gloomy forebodings.—The changed demeanor of some women after conception.—The husband's duty in such cases.—The wife should become intelligent before conception takes place.—The husband should secure intelligence by reading the best books.—Valuable suggestions on diet, rest and exercise from "Trained Motherhood."—Mistakes often made after confinement.—The marital relation during pregnancy.—The example of birds and animals.—The custom in heathen countries.—Medical authorities quoted.—Importance of an undisturbed maternity, ... 197

CHAPTER XIV.

THE CHANGES WHICH PRECEDE, ATTEND AND FOLLOW CHILDBIRTH.

Wonderful adaptation of body of the mother to reproduction.—How wonderful a watch which could oil, repair and produce other watches, and keep accurate time.—Wonders of reproduction seen in the flower.—Death defeated and extinction prevented by reproduction.—The agony of splendor which attends the period of fertilization of the flowers.—After fertilization the flower fades.—Similar changes in human life.—Illustrated in the birds.—The changes in appearance and demeanor more marked in the female.—The greater changes within the mother's body.—How conception takes place.—Why two parents instead of one.—The womb seems almost instinct with intelligence.—No spermatozoön or ovum retained unless the two have united.—The changes which take place in the ovum.—Its reception and royal cradle in the womb.—The cradle enlarged with the growth of its occupant.—In the minute egg are ingrained the characteristics of the man or woman that is to be.—How the germ is at first nourished.—The formation of the placenta and its office, ... 216

CHAPTER XV.

THE CHANGES WHICH PRECEDE, ATTEND AND FOLLOW CHILDBIRTH.
(Continued.)

The formation of the sacs about the germ of life.—Spontaneous segmentation.—Formation of Blastodermic membrane.—The embryonic spot.—The different membranes which enclose the embryo.—The gathering of "the waters," or the amniotic fluid.—The office of the amniotic fluid.—The growth of the embryo described by Dr. Guernsey.—The rudimentary embryo at five weeks, at seven weeks, two months, and ten weeks.—At end of the fifth month the embryo known as the fetus.—Changes indicated at time of birth.—Man fearfully and wonderfully made.—Bodily changes of the mother as parturition approaches.—The descent of the womb.—Enlargement of vagina and external parts.—The coming away of "the plug," or "the show."—Premonitory pains.—Undue apprehensions of danger.—Wonderful changes that take place in the body of the mother at birth of child.—Changes in the body of the child after its birth, . 233

CHAPTER XVI.

WHEN THE BABY IS BORN.

Birth at tenth menstrual period.—Labor-pains and after-pains.—Intelligent preparation removes anxiety and danger.—What the husband needs to know if no physician is present.—Severing of placentic cord.—The physician's instructions to be obeyed.—Should the husband remain with his wife?—The afterbirth.—The first need of the child.—The care of the mother.—Protection from visitors.—The selection of a nurse.—From six weeks to three months to secure normal condition of reproductive organs.—Marital relation after confinement and miscarriage.—Instances of cruel exactions.—Nature of first nourishment of child.—Dangers of wet-nurses and vicious nurse-girls.—The pleasures of fatherhood.—The father's duty to his children, ... 251

PART III.

CONCERNING HIS CHILDREN.

CHAPTER XVII.

HEREDITY.

Only early knowledge can be of any benefit to offspring.—Our previous treatment of heredity.—The three periods of greatest molding power.—Relation of correct model to finished statue.—Education of child begins "twenty years before it is born."—Heredity in horses.—Effect of mental state of mother upon the forming unborn offspring.—Emotions effect chemical changes in the breath. — Physical and mental state effect exhalations of body.—Odors of insane asylums, penitentiaries, etc.—Achievements in development of domestic animals, birds, fruit trees, flowers, etc.—These laws in human heredity.—Modifying interferences.—" Degenerate sons of noble sires."—Causes not difficult to find.—Essentials of good soil, good seed and good care, . . 265

CHAPTER XVIII.

PRENATAL INFLUENCES.

Prenatal influences illustrated.—Robert Burns, Napoleon. — A kleptomaniac. — How some murderers were made.—Guiteau.—The mother of an artist.—The twins that liked books.—Various instances named.—Child-marking.—

A child with two thumbs.—Born with but one hand.—Corrective theory of C. J. Bayer.—Corrective longings.—"Longings."—Their treatment.—Their effects.—Instances given.—The mother's molding power in producing characteristics desired in her children.—Potency of this influence.—Forming versus reforming.—A word of comfort to parents of children that are marked at birth.—Diverse theories concerning the determining of sex, 276

CHAPTER XIX.

CHILDHOOD.

The opportunities for forming and reforming during infancy.—Books and periodicals on nurture and training of children.—Importance of first two years.—Evils of promiscuous kissing.—Potency of nursery influences.—Protecting the child from vices of servants.—Danger from secret vice.—Honest answers to honest inquiries.—Forestall degrading information from vicious companions.—The parents' duty at puberty of child.—Education of children.—Their physical culture.—Moral training.—The parting word, 290

PREFACE.

IN approaching the work which we have undertaken in these pages, we have not been blind to the difficulties which confront us in entering upon so delicate a subject. If we had thought only of these, we would never have taken up our pen in this work. We have been moved to it by the cries of disappointment and anguish which may be heard everywhere throughout our land, and by the pleadings that come up out of the dense ignorance which envelops palace and hovel alike. Knowing the importance of these "matters which are so central in our physical life, so essential in their relation to the condition, character, career and destiny of every ndividual, and so fundamental and vital to every institution and interest of society;" knowing also the importance of proper intelligence concerning the laws which govern our bodies, and knowing how the honest and the pure who seek information concerning these most sacred relations of human life are exposed, amid the dearth of pure and reliable books, to contamination by books whose secret character designedly fosters the very lusts and evils which they are professedly written to denounce, we have felt that we would be recreant to duty, to humanity and to God if we allowed difficulties to bar us from this important work. Turn where you will, the manifest consequences of the prevalent ignorance upon these vital and important subjects stare one in the face, and the appealing need of the hosts of honest men and women who desire such information as will enable them to attain the noblest and the best which God has placed within their reach is a sufficient condemnation of that spurious "modesty" which desires that a ban shall continue upon intelligence, so that men and women may remain in a hopeless bondage to vice and its awful consequences.

Knowing the universal need for the information which we have sought to communicate in a plain and pure way in these pages, and while laboring with an ever-present sense of the difficulties and delicacies of the undertaking, we have turned to our task with greater assurance when we have remembered the appreciative messages of eminent men and women which have come from all quarters of the globe, the unreserved and hearty commendations which the earlier books of the series have received from the entire religious, secular, educational and medical press of the United States, England and Canada; we have been inspired by the fact that these books are already being translated into other languages; that without suggestion they have been publicly commended at the different international conventions of Christian workers in this country, and are also being used by Christian missionaries in many lands in their efforts to redeem and save the heathen.

To many, marriage is not that source of blessing and happiness which God intended. Its purposes and possibilities are never realized. Thousands are constantly entering upon marriage only to be miserable and wretched because they do not understand the nature and intent of their own endowments, or the purpose of God in ordaining the institution. Whatever information they ever obtain is secured by blind blunderings, and at the most ruinous cost. Even where no permanent physical consequences are entailed, mental and moral effects, which are even more ruinous in their results, remain to mar the blessings of later years. Had they been intelligent, they might have possessed from the very first the benefits and blessings which ignorance has placed and kept beyond their reach. Sad as such results are, they are still more grievous because of the consequences which must be suffered by their families, and which are handed down to innocent children who are to reap the results of parental ignorance long years after the parents themselves may have passed away. It is to save young men and young women from such disastrous and far-reaching results, and to afford them the blessing and happiness which God intended, that we have set ourselves to the task undertaken in these pages.

To secure the largest assistance from these pages, it is necessary to know that this book is supplemental and stands related to the two which have preceded in the nature of an educational series. To comprehend the entire subject of the reproductive organs, their purpose, function and preservation, it would be well also to know the contents of the books which follow this present volume in the same series.

Gratefully acknowledging the valuable aid and assistance from many sources, trustfully seeking the continued co-operation of the good and pure everywhere, and relying upon the favor and blessing of Him whose guidance we have constantly sought, this volume is now sent forth on its important mission.

SYLVANUS STALL.

PHILADELPHIA, PA.,
 July 20, 1899.

PART 1
CONCERNING HIMSELF

WHAT A YOUNG HUSBAND OUGHT TO KNOW.

CHAPTER I.

THE RELATION OF MARRIAGE.

THE young man who marries finds himself in an entirely new relation in life. Grand as life may have been in the past, the present and the future are full of new meaning, of grander possibilities and of larger blessing. God has meant that love should come to man to glorify life and to lift the lower nature of husband and wife into higher realms of thought and being; to transform, deepen, broaden and soften. In them love becomes the potent source of mightiest inspirations. The husband's duty seemed formerly to be to care, to arrange and to provide only for himself. Now he has assumed additional responsibilities. He is no longer to live for himself, but for his wife, his children, and in a larger sense for his descendants—for the good of the race. He is to continue by transmitting himself, that life may remain when he is gone. What he does involves the interests of his wife, and of those who are to come after him. Love is to conquer selfishness. He is to rise above himself, and the present good and future happiness of others are to constitute his well-being.

His present and future happiness will be dependent upon a clear apprehension of the fact that what he is will determine what his descendants are to be after him. He should comprehend the fullest meaning of what is taught in the statement that "we are part of all the people whom we have met," the result of past influences and previous life. What we have been and are, that we transmit. The responsibilities are grave, but the state of two congenial souls made one in happy marriage is the grandest and most blessed earthly condition conferred upon man by God himself. It meets the requirements of our being, and, when properly understood and faithfully conformed to, brings the largest happiness that mortals are capable of upon earth. Husband and wife, parents and child, home and country, form the centre of all that makes life dear.

The purest, noblest and most unselfish aspirations and purposes derive their strength and being from the sweet influences which have their beginning and their continuance in this power which draws men and women together in happy and holy wedlock. By these sweet influences the most perfect natures are moulded and ennobled. By them are formed the strongest ties that hold humanity to the accomplishment of every high and holy endeavor. Where the mind has continued pure, and the character untarnished, and the life unsullied by the touch of social evil, the sexual impulse does not die in that cradle of our being where God has given it birth but marches like a mighty conqueror, arousing and marshalling the mightiest human forces in every department of man's nature. It formulates his purpose, quickens his imagination, and calls into exercise his united powers in the attainment of the world's greatest and grandest achievements in art, in letters, in inventions, in philosophy, in philanthropy, and in every effort that is to secure the universal blessing of mankind.

It is under the awakening of the reproductive life that the fields put on their verdure, the flowers unfold their beauty and fragrance, the birds put on their brightest plumage and sing their sweetest song, while the chirp of the cricket, the note of the katydid, is but the call to its mate—for the many-tongued voices which break the stillness of field and forest are but the myriad notes of love. To this universal, God-given passion, man owes his love of color, his love of beauty and sweetness in art and music, his love of rhythm in poetry, of grace in form, in painting, in sculpture; and from it not only springs the love of the beautiful, but even the perception and recognition of all that which is pleasing and lovely.

This is the emotion that strengthens every faculty, quickens every power, animates, modifies, ennobles, purifies and sweetens the entire being, and makes our life upon earth, when directed by godly purposes, the unfolding and enriching of those nobler powers of the soul which are to find their fullest fruition and perfection in heaven itself.

While these powers may all be kept in abeyance until financial, social, religious and other requirements can be adequately met, yet there is a proper time for their full expression and purposed exercise. While God has meant that reason should rule over passion, and that every sexual impulse should yield to other requirements and activities, yet He has wisely purposed that these leadings of our nature should be pronounced and strong. If these sentiments and emotions were not strong—very strong indeed—no man, knowing the risks and dangers which are liable to arise because of incompatibility of temper, mistaken estimates of physical, intellectual and moral qualifications, would take upon himself the responsibilities, incur the risks, augment his expenses, and assume the far-reaching obligations which are involved when two are united, "for better or for worse," in indissoluble bonds for life.

Were not the sentiment and emotions strong in woman, as well as in man, what woman would assume the responsibilities of wife and mother? Whatever man is required to give up, to endure, to suffer, to risk, even more seems to fall to the lot of woman. Were it not for strong sentiment and moving emotion, what woman would commit her entire future to the keeping of any man? Where is one who would assume the pains and perils of maternity, with the subsequent possibility of being left by the death of her husband with a family of dependent children?

If the young husband desires in marriage the joys and blessings with which God has crowned this relation, he need not seek the immolation of his sexual nature, but he does need to subordinate his sexual passion to the reign of reason and the government of the moral sense. He cannot afford to ignore the rights, the comfort and the wishes of his wife. If he looks upon marriage as an easy means of securing self-indulgence, as affording a safe and lawful means for unbridled gratification, he is doomed to disappointment and to misery. If passion is to be enthroned where God ordained that none but love should reign, then anarchy with all its attendant horrors must, and surely will, desolate the heart, the home and the life; for lust can filch but cannot enjoy the pleasures and blessings of this heaven-ordained relation, which are reserved only for the pure, who live under the domain and rule of love and reason.

To comprehend love in its intended relation to sexual impulse, and at the same time to understand something of it in its diviner aspects; to know love in its beauty, greatness and power; to free it from ideas of grossness and evil, and yet to retain in healthful balance and poise that portion of our nature which God has assigned so prominent and so important a place in man's estate of present happiness and the future prosperity and blessing of the race, is the instant duty of all intelligent men and women, both young and old. Conscientiously to relate these emotions of our nature to the highest well-being of the individual and the race, and to redeem the purest and most sacred relation of life from the realm of degradation and shame, to disarm and depose that sensual usurper which has been enthroned and worshiped in the name of love, and "set love herself upon the throne, fair, luminous and pure," to gladden, to bless, and to save, shall be both our effort and our justification.

CHAPTER II.

DIFFERENCES OF SEX.

IT is both difficult and unnecessary to determine which is the superior of the two sexes. When the subject is regarded in its true light there is no superiority upon the part of either, and at the same time each is superior to the other in the sphere in which God designed them to move. The truth was perhaps aptly represented by President Lincoln when presented at the same time with two hats by rival hatters. Both hats were about as perfect as it was possible for human skill to make them. He desired to recognize this perfection in both, and yet to avoid discrimination in favor of either, and in that matchless sufficiency which qualified him for the demands of almost any situation, Mr. Lincoln, in accepting the hats, said: "Gentlemen, your hats mutually excel each other." The same is true of men and women; they mutually excel each other. In man's place, he is superior; and in woman's place, she is superior. The wisdom with which God has adapted each for the important place which they are to occupy in life is well worth our thought and study, and a clear apprehension of the subject will help to remove many of the misunderstandings, estrangements and conflicts which so frequently arise in married life.

That neither is superior to the other, but that they are two parts of one complete whole, segments of the same circle, and that their union is absolutely essential to unity and entirety, will be best understood as we study what these differences are. In some respects man is inferior to woman, while in other respects woman is inferior to man. In a happy marriage these differences become complemental, rendering possible that superior unity in which the two are made one. Let us note what some of these differences are.

In stature, woman is shorter than man. In the United States the average height of men is about five feet eight inches, and the weight about one hundred and forty-five pounds. The average woman is about five feet three inches in height, and about one hundred and twenty-five pounds in weight. The normally-developed man has broad shoulders and narrow hips, while woman has narrow shoulders and broad hips. Her shoulders set further back, giving her breast greater depth. In effecting this change her collar-bone is shorter, and this is one reason why she cannot throw a stone or ball with as much accuracy as man. In man the muscles are well defined, and indicate great strength, while in woman, even when the muscles are well developed, the outlines are more hidden by fatty and cellular tissues, which fill all the hollows and round off all angles, giving her peculiar grace and beauty. He has greater muscular force, but she has more power of endurance. The bony structure of woman is smaller, and more delicately formed. The angles of the bones are less projecting, and the joints better concealed. The skull is smaller, and the bones of the cranium thinner. The sternum, or breastbone, is shorter and flatter, and the clavicles, or collar-bones, more crooked and shorter. His voice is deeper and more guttural; hers softer and more musical. Her neck is longer, her skin softer, her hair less generally diffused but more luxuriant in growth than in man.

The most noticeable feature in the study of the differences of the bony structure of the two sexes is observable in the pelvis—a word derived from the Greek, signifying dish or bowl. In man this structure is simply to subserve the purposes of strength and motion. In woman this bony basin, which forms the lower part of the body, has an additional purpose of special importance. At her side the hip-bones form the highest points, and from these the pelvis slopes down until in front it forms a comparatively narrow rim called the pubic arch. This change of form in woman is designed to adapt her body to become the first cradle of her children, and in the fullness of time to permit the easy transit of a new being into the outer world. In preparing woman for maternity, God has thus equipped her with such physical adaptation as is suited to the carrying of her temporary burden, while at the same time affording protection for the hidden life within, thus fitting the physical frame of woman to the mother-nature with which He has endowed her.

While woman is thus furnished with physical requisites suited to the easiest accomplishment of the divine purpose—while the form of her body, the articulation of her bones and the size of her muscles all indicate her sense of dependence upon man—God has, with like wisdom, adapted man in all of his physical endowments to become the shield and defender of woman. He is to be her protection and her defense. His fiercer visage, his broader shoulders, his more muscular frame, all speak clearly of the divine purpose.

Intellectually, as well as physically, men and women are best suited for their respective duties and responsibilities in life. In arriving at a conclusion, man is much more deliberate and logical, proceeding step by step after an orderly method; while woman reaches the conclusion in much less time by means of her intuition. While woman is by no means incapable of logical deductions, yet generally she does not stop to reason it out, but takes refuge in the statement that she "knows that it is so;" that she is "sure that she is right." It is easy to see that intellectually, as well as physically, men and women are complemental, and when the conclusions arrived at are identical they become confirmatory of each other. While men would be likely to prefer the conclusions which are reached by their own method, yet women in the exercise of the same freedom are likely to prefer the intuitions of their own sex. For either to decide in favor of the intellectual superiority of their own sex would be somewhat like the case of two men engaged in a lawsuit, where one takes it upon himself to become umpire and decide in favor of himself and against his opponent.

The nervous system of woman is more refined and more delicate than that in man. This greater nervous sensibility renders her more susceptible to impressions, enables her to dwell constantly in the realm of more refined susceptibilities, rendering distasteful to her all things that are coarse and low, and at the same time endowing her with a greater capacity both for pleasure and for pain. Man's sources of pleasure are not always hers, but in love of her home and its adornment, in love of her children and their well-being, of literature, art, music and religion, she usually surpasses man, save in exceptional cases.

To enable woman, with her finer nervous sensibilities, to meet the larger burden of pain and suffering which is laid upon her, God has adequately fitted her by bestowing a compensating power of endurance. If we desire to deny woman this greater sensitiveness and greater endurance we would need to ignore the patience and bravery with which they face and bear the pains and perils of maternity—pains and sufferings of which they assert that man cannot form the remotest idea.

But there are also other differences less manifest to the superficial observer, but none the less real and important to those who would comprehend the wonderful wisdom of the Creator and intelligently prepare themselves to receive the good which is designed for and is possible to intelligent men and women.

There are inherent differences of character and modifications of temperament which can be best understood by studying the very earliest manifestations of human life when we examine the sperm of the male and the ovum of the female as seen under the microscope. These characteristics are not imaginary, but inherent, and are manifestly designed and intended by the all-wise Creator. And it is only when we study these characteristics in their entirety, with a desire to understand the divine purpose, that we can measurably comprehend how these individual differences in each contribute to the blessing and the well-being of both.

The part contributed by the mother in the reproductive act toward the life of the future child is called an ovum, which means an egg; for all forms of life, both vegetable and animal, begin with a seed or egg, which are two names for the same thing. In the lower forms of life these eggs are usually produced on the exterior of the plant, while in the higher forms of life, as, for instance, in the bird, the seed or egg is produced in the inside of the body, and after being perfected is expelled, to be hatched in a nest, where the young, when they attain their proper size, break the shell and emerge into the outer world. In the highest forms of life the ovum reaches its maturity in a department of the mother's body which is called the ovary. In woman, at the end of a period of twenty-eight days, as a succeeding ovum ripens it passes into a tube which awaits its reception, and is moved onward into the womb, where it remains for a period, awaiting the reception of the male element called the spermatozoa. This is the plural, while a single one is called a spermatozoön. The ovum or egg of the mother is so small that two hundred and forty of them would need to be laid side by side in order to make a row one inch long. The spermatozoön, the principle of life contributed by the male, is so small that it is not visible to the eye except by the aid of a microscope, and, when seen, somewhat resembles a pollywog. These minute centres of life are alive, and move in a fluid which is secreted by the male organs of reproduction, and which is generally called semen. Now, if we study the characteristics of the ovum and of the spermatozoön we may be surprised when we discover some of the same differences which characterize men and women from infancy to old age.

In passing through the tube which is to carry it into the womb from that portion of the body of the mother where it has attained its growth and perfection, the ovum is passive—does not move by its own inherent life, but is carried forward to its designed place by the movement in the tube itself, the same as the food which is masticated in the mouth is passed on to the stomach, not by any action in the food itself, but by the movement of the esophagus, which passes it onward to its destined place in the stomach. In other words, the ovum is passive.

When we come to the spermatozoa, or sperm, of the male, we find an entirely different manifestation. Just the same as you see the pollywog moving in the water, or tiny fish swimming about in the pool, so the spermatozoa move with activity and vigor in the semen, and when this has been transferred to the interior of the body of the mother in the manner in which God designed, it retains its activity, moving vigorously about in the upper portion of the vaginal cavity until it finds the entrance into the womb. Passing through and above the cervix, it continues to move about with great activity until it finds an ovum, which it seeks with avidity. When it reaches the womb, if there is no ovum present, it may remain there for a period of days awaiting its arrival, or may find its way into one of the Fallopian tubes which lead out to the ovary, and even go in quest of the object of its search as far as the ovary itself. These little creatures, one-fortieth of an inch in length, and requiring that hundreds of them should be laid side by side in order to extend one single inch, are so numerous that hundreds of them exist in a single drop of semen, and yet a single one is all that is necessary in order to fertilize the ovum and render complete the beginning of a new life.

While the ovum is passive, the sperm of the male is characterized by great activity and remarkable vitality. Dr. Napheys says: "The secretive fluid has been frozen and kept at a temperature of zero during four days, yet when it was thawed, these animalcules, as they are supposed to be, were as active as ever." In her interesting book, entitled "Life and Love," Margaret Warner Morley says: "Under the microscope these active forms have been seen eagerly moving around and around the egg until one, more fortunate than the rest, finds admission and dissolves into the substance of the egg—not to be finally lost, however, for, as we know, this inexplicable union results in the growth of a new creature like neither parent, and yet like both, each cell having given to the new life certain characteristics of the creature from which it was derived."

This greater activity of the sperm is seen also at the birth of the child; for physicians tell us that the pulse of a male child at birth beats two or three times a minute faster than that of a female child. The tissues of the male are also characterized by the same superior activity; and not only among men, but among all creatures. The tissues of the male have a greater tendency to change than those of the female. In the very fibre of her structure she is quiet, while he is more active.

Characterized by this more marked vitality, more sturdy form and more muscular frame, we would naturally expect that the vitality of male children would be greater than that of female children. But this is not the case. It is claimed by some good authorities that about five per cent. more male than female children are born into the world, but at five years of age more girls are alive than boys.

And what may seem increasingly strange, when we consider the greater perils to which the life of women is exposed in child-bearing, the "expectation of life," as life-insurance companies designate it, is greater in woman than in man, and when the census of old persons is taken, the larger number of them are women.

The civil law recognizes this more passive nature of females and the more intense activity of males by regarding the man as the criminal in all actions for fornication or bastardy. While public sentiment ostracizes and is more severe and unrelenting with the woman, the law always inflicts its penalty upon the man.

CHAPTER III.

DIFFERENCES OF SEX.

Continued.

THESE differences in temperament indicate the infinite wisdom of the Creator, and to any thoughtful observer the many benefits must be manifest. Longfellow, in his "Hiawatha," says:

> "As unto the bow the cord is,
> So unto the man is woman.
> Though she bends him, she obeys him;
> Though she draws him, yet she follows:
> Useless each without the other."

Woman might be said to be, both in the family and in society, the centripetal force, insuring permanency, attracting and drawing to herself and within herself, thus preventing, in the family and in society, the tendency to fly from the centre and to produce chaos. Man is life's centrifugal force. The impetuosity and velocity of his nature tend to throw everything from the centre. His influence is to prevent gravitation from drawing everything to a given point, where all would become a state of rest. While woman keeps life stable, man keeps it from stagnation; but it requires the reciprocal influence of each to secure that harmony which God intended. Woman's stability unmodified by man's influence would tend to result in complete rest, which would mean stagnation and death. Man's greater impetuosity would lead to instability, unrest, and possible chaos. As, in nature, the centrifugal and centripetal forces equalize and balance themselves, swaying the spheres in fixed orbits, so the influences of men and women upon each other, both in the family and in society, help to secure and maintain an even balance. While opposite in tendency, they are yet of equal necessity and of equal value. Each is essential to the perfection and completeness of the other, and perfect unity is only secured by the union of the two.

The reciprocal influences of men and women are oftentimes noticed in old couples who have passed thirty or forty years together in peace and harmony, each living year after year under the moulding power of the other, and each being moulded by the surroundings and influences which have wrought upon the other. Year after year they become more alike in form, feature and expression. Their views and opinions become increasingly harmonized, until there comes also to be a mental resemblance. That they have lived in the midst of the same surroundings and breathed the same air, have eaten the same kind of food, have shared each other's joys and pleasures, have laughed and wept together, have been under the formative influences of the same conditions, tend in a measure to this increasing likeness; but under the reciprocal influences each has lost a portion of this more pronounced personality and taken upon himself or herself the physical, intellectual and moral features of the other. Their union has constantly tended to unity.

In religious matters there is also a noticeable difference between men and women. Generally, woman responds more readily to religious teachings and influences, and by nature she manifestly follows the Master's leadings more closely than her male companion; and there are good reasons evident why this should be so. With the uninterrupted duties of the household, which are oftentimes even multiplied on Sundays, it is necessary that a moral sense correspondingly more acute should prompt her to overcome the difficulties which beset her in her approach to the sanctuary, and God has given her that added moral force which is designed to enable her to overcome the increased resistance which she meets in the performance of her religious duties. There are times also when, in the discharge of her special duties as wife and mother, for weeks, and even for months, she is called upon to minister to others in sickness, or give herself to the care of infant children; and were it not for the larger endowment of her devotional nature, these repeated and prolonged but enforced absences from God's house would result in the formation of a fixed habit which would eventually wholly keep the majority of women from attendance upon all religious assemblies.

But in view of the important fact that God

has more largely entrusted the moral and religious training of the children to the mother, we need to think but for a moment to understand what would be the result if her own nature was not endowed with sufficient strength to enable her to overcome every barrier, and to rise to the higher plane of duty and responsibility in this matter. The exceptional instances of mothers who are themselves deficient in their moral nature and neglectful of religious duties, and who, on that account, fail utterly in the moral and religious training of their children, are quite sufficient to illustrate what would be the condition in the home, in the Church, the community, and the State, if God had not endowed woman with a stronger moral nature and a keener sense of religious obligation than is found in man. It is by this more active moral sense in woman that the religious poise and balance of the family is maintained; and its benign results are often seen, not only in the children, but in the husband as well.

The complemental differences in the intellectual and moral natures of men and women are as essential to the highest and best development of the entire nature of each as the complemental physical and sexual differences of each are indispensable to that union in which the two are made one in the child which is begotten of the father and born of the mother.

This reflexive and reciprocal influence of each sex upon the other to the mutual modification and advantage of both is clearly seen in the nation, as well as in the life of the family. This thought is beautifully presented by Margaret Warner Morley in her book entitled "Life and Love": "In the lower life, and in savages, the community in its characteristics approaches the masculine type; it is selfish, egoistic, unstable, variable. The herd of buffalo, for illustration, roams about in search of food and water, charging relentlessly and destroying whatever enemy comes in its way. The savage tribe often has no fixed abode, but roams about from place to place; where it has a home it is, as a rule, given to frequent war with its neighbors, and is liable to be uprooted by a stronger foe and absorbed, and thus lost, or it may be destroyed or compelled to move on. While this is true in the savage community *as a whole*, that is, considered as a nation, a unit; in its internal organization, on the other hand, it is essentially *feminine* in its characteristics; its habits are simple, stable, not liable to change. It makes no inventions, elaborates no complex machinery."

In civilized life, the opposite characteristics predominate. The community as a whole constantly takes upon itself the best characteristics of the feminine type. It becomes stable, less given to change. It does not seek war, but prefers peace, becomes more and more quiescent and altruistic.

While these external changes are discernible, corresponding changes take place in the *internal* national life. The civilized nation tends to move away from the feminine toward the masculine type. Inventions and innovations constantly change the order of things. National existence is established, but the existence of the individual calls for a more vigorous struggle. Competitions become fierce, and the struggle between labor and capital becomes more intense, and the exertion of personal energy merges into an effort to secure prestige and place, wealth and power; consequently the higher faculties generally obtain their larger development.

In this approach toward the feminine type the community as a whole parts with some of its less desirable masculine expressions; it becomes modified, less angular. The desire for war departs, courage remains, and energy finds expression in new and nobler directions. But while these changes are taking place, the community does not discard all its masculine characteristics. It simply parts with the lower or least desirable of each, while the best elements of both are united in the new manifestation.

To quote further from Miss Morley's interesting paragraphs: "Certain changes which mark the advanced community as a whole, necessarily, and in no less degree, mark the individuals composing it. The sexes are not sharply distinguished from each other in the intellectual and emotional realms. On the whole, men as a class probably show a preponderance of what may be termed masculine characteristics, as greater egoism, variability, activity; but these masculine characteristics have been modified, lessened, *effeminized*, so to speak. In the higher type of man the best and highest feminine characteristics have been fused with the best and highest masculine characteristics. The fighting instinct, for instance, has become moral courage; the tendency to vary expresses itself in great intellectual development; instability and restlessness have become intellectual rather than physical qualities, leading to notable inventions and discoveries.

"Brave and gentle, strong and tender, inventive and patient, the finest type of man owes his superiority to the transforming and illuminating power of his inheritance of womanly qualities.

"In the higher type of woman the best and highest masculine characteristics have been fused with the best and highest development of the feminine characteristics. Altruism, for instance, has been rationalized and guarded by the exercise of greater reasoning power; stability, or inertia, has been lessened and prevented from forming an insurmountable barrier to progress. The tendency to vary has been strengthened; the more negative nature has progressed to a more positive condition. Courage, inventiveness and greater strength of intellectual perception have been fostered in civilized woman. Her submission to man gradually lessens before the upward progress of her mind. She places herself as his equal—as the other half, without which his half-life cannot be complete.

"Nor does this borrowing of the characteristics of each by the other mean the merging of the two sexes into one,—the obliteration of sex difference, and hence of sex attraction. It means the elevation of man by developing his masculine qualities in the direction of their highest possibilities, and by adding to manhood a new charm, a subtle grace, an irresistible beauty. It means the elevation of woman by the development of her womanly qualities in the direction of their highest possibilities, and by adding to womanhood a new power, a deeper, more far-reaching sympathy, an ineffable glow and a nobler beauty.

"The mind is a mighty solvent; through it the two sexes have been united in an intellectual union, from which has been born a new man with the dominant masculine characteristics developed in the noblest direction, and enriched by union with feminine characteristics, and a new woman with the feminine characteristics grandly developed and enhanced by what was once in the province of masculine knowledge and activity."

In harmony with what we have been considering in this chapter, it is eminently proper to discuss briefly the reciprocal sexual tempers and tendencies of married men and women. While the discussion of the various modifications of these differences does not belong to this chapter, yet the recognition of the fact itself and a noting of the beneficial, reactionary and reciprocal effects are pre-eminently in place just at this point.

The active nature of the sperm of the male and the passivity which distinguishes the ovum of the female characterize the two sexes from the beginning to the end of their existence. The greater activity of the sperm, the quickened pulse of the male child at birth, the more restless nature of the boy-baby, his running, climbing, active life throughout childhood and adolescence—these traits characterize not only his boyhood, his days of developing manhood, but his marital relations as well.

With rare exceptions, both of person and of instances, in married life all the sexual aggressiveness is with the male. Wives seldom seek the closer embraces of their husbands. They are generally indifferent; often absolutely averse. With the husband, while in perfect health, the conditions are quite the opposite; and the wisdom of the Creator is manifest in the fact that were the wife equally quickened by the same amative tendencies, the male nature would be called into such frequent and continuous exercise that the power of reproduction would be either totally destroyed or so impaired that the race would degenerate into moral, intellectual and physical pigmies. God has made the passivity of the wife the protection of her husband and a source of manifold blessing to their children.

Upon the other hand, her uninterrupted and entire neglect of the sexual relation is wisely overcome, to the advantage of the wife, by her husband's greater sexual activity, while at the same time her restraining passiveness is made his safeguard and security. Each brings into the married relation inclinations and propensities which are to modify the other, to the mutual benefit of both.

If husbands and wives only knew and adequately realized these facts, and harmonized their thought and conduct toward each other accordingly, much of the discord, estrangement and consequent unhappiness in married life would be eliminated and disappear. When both alike recognize these differences and the Wisdom which has made them to differ, and when each is willing to accept the modifying influence of the other in the manner in which God has intended, the discord and misery which blight thousands of lives and destroy such multitudes of homes will give place to a benediction and blessing which will restore to earth a larger measure of the happiness of Eden.

But before closing this chapter upon the complemental differences between the two sexes, it will be interesting to observe some remarkable similarities in the reproductive organs themselves, and to note how, in that infinite wisdom which is marvelous in our eyes, God has so modified their form and office that the external organs of reproduction in man become the internal and seemingly different organs of reproduction in woman.

To understand the full significance of what we have briefly to say upon this subject it will be well to recall the fact that in man and animals even those physical characteristies which may be regarded as strictly feminine are present in a rudimentary form in the male, and *vice versa*. Let a single instance suffice. The paps and breasts of the male are but the diminutive and dormant breasts and nipples of the female; and this is true not only with man, but with the lower animals.

The male not only simulates but really possesses in rudimentary form all the parts and powers which characterize the fuller development in the opposite sex.

That this is true is demonstrated by the cases of abnormal sexual development which at long intervals are born in different lands, and by the occasional instances in heathen countries where old men, after prolonged stimulation of the breasts, are made effectively to serve as nurses for infants.

As the pelvic bone in man and woman is modified by the various changes of form which adapt it to the different necessities of each sex, so in a large measure are the reproductive organs, primarily, the same in men and women.

If you enlarge the curve of the pelvic frontal, then press the scrotum or sack of the male upward into the body, it will correspond to the vagina and the womb of the female. Move the testicles to the right and the left and you have their counterparts, the ovaries, while the spermatic cords form the Fallopian tubes for the passage of the completely formed ovum from the ovaries to the womb. Without materially disturbing its position, diminish the sexual member of the male and you have the clitoris of the female.

It is readily seen that with these changes of position, together with slight modifications of form and function, those parts which to the unobservant and the unthoughtful seem wholly different in the two sexes are, after all, discovered to be only diversified forms of the same thing.

But this very fact, however, invests the study of this subject with increased interest, and displays in an unexpected manner the wonderful wisdom which characterizes everything that God has created; for as these organs take upon themselves the modifications of either sex, every other organ and faculty that together constitute the individual must be so modified as to adjust the physical, intellectual, social and moral natures into harmonious unity of personality.

CHAPTER IV.

ESSENTIALS IN HUSBAND AND HOME.

Before writing of what a young husband ought to know with regard to his wife and his children, subjects which are to engage our thought in Part Second and Part Third, it is important that we should carefully consider some matters which he ought to know concerning himself; for his future happiness, and usefulness as well, will be quite as much dependent upon the mental, physical and moral equipment which he personally brings to the union as the endowments and qualifications which are possessed by his partner and companion.

If your wife is to have a fair chance for a pleasant home and a happy and useful life, she will need a husband who can sacrifice his personal luxuries and self-indulgences in order that he may share with her and the family the comforts and blessings of their home—a man who will scorn the saloon, avoid the club, remain away from the lodge, give up his cigar, and spend his time and his money for the comfort and happiness of his family.

There are hundreds of homes which are rendered unhappy, and in many senses miserable, because of the neglect and want which are due wholly to the selfishness and lack of consideration upon the part of the husband. If you wish to preserve and perpetuate that which is noblest and best in your wife and your children, you can only do so by making your home the centre of your thought, and by making your loved ones the sharers of your purse and your pleasures. If you wish them to live for your comfort and happiness, they have an equal right to expect you to live and sacrifice for their comfort and happiness. Almost any promising bride may soon be made an ill-tempered wife, a discontented homekeeper and an indifferent mother by an improvident, extravagant, selfish and neglectful husband. In most instances, ruined homes come principally from drink, idleness, bad temper, shiftlessness and thriftless habits, brutal husbands, slatternly wives and Christless living. Do your duty faithfully to your wife and your children, and then, if home and happiness are wrecked, the responsibility will not rest upon you.

In woman, the love of home is usually more dominant than in man. By cultivating this in yourself you will produce a harmony of thought and purpose which will contribute greatly to the comfort and well-being of both. Adorn your home with your own hands. Beautify the lawn, the shrubbery, and all external surroundings. It matters not how great your wealth, or how small your purse, every consideration, effort and sacrifice you make in these directions will add to your own health and happiness and endear you to your wife. In the development of this common interest, you may secure in your own experience and the experience of your wife that happiness which is so manifest in springtime in the united industry of the two robins as they mold and fashion the nest together, moved by a common impulse and the premonition of the birdlings that are soon to be.

Be devoted. Keep up your courtship. Remember and repeat the little attentions which gave you pleasure months and years ago simply because you knew that they were a source of pleasure to the one whom you coveted as your bride and companion for life. How can your wife love and respect you if you neglect and forsake her? During your courtship, the club, the lodge and the society of others had to accept second place. You preferred her company to that of all others. If you are to her and she to you what each should be, this preference of the one for the society and companionship of the other will continue throughout life. Your home will be your clubhouse, and no society, or gilded hall, or corner grocery with its lounging company, will be able to attract you from her and from your home.

Most men who frequent these places are attracted there; but some go there because repelled from their homes. There are women whose inconsiderate treatment of their husbands repels them from their families and their homes, and the husbands simply resort to the club or other place of assemblage in their natural search for a place of refuge and fellowship. But such instances are the exception. In the majority of cases the fault is largely, if not wholly, with the husband. Oftentimes his conduct is due to his thoughtlessness, but more frequently to pure selfishness.

Recently the writer called at the home of a mechanic to secure his services in a job of work. It was between eight and nine o'clock in the evening, and quite dark. For some time no one answered our knock. Finally a young wife, looking pale, weary and lonely, bearing a large lamp in one hand and a small child on the other arm, opened the door of the desolate home. We had a right to expect to find the husband and father at home, but no; to our inquiry we were told that we would likely find him at the toll-gate, the harness-maker's, or the grocery. Unless indications were deceptive, here was a case of cold indifference and selfish neglect. Would that this were a rare instance; but there are thousands of such in all circles of society in our cities and towns, and in the country as well.

We clip the following suggestive incident, and submit it as pertinent at this place:

"'My home shall be my clubhouse' said a young, unmarried, traveling-man, when returning from a visit to a former friend who had married and lived in a pleasant home. Almost the first words the latter spoke, as his visitor seated himself in the parlor, was: 'I want you to go over with me and see our nice, new club-rooms.'"

"But I did not come to see them," was the reply; "I came to see you and your family."

"That you can do anyhow," was the response, "so please get ready and we will go over and spend the evening there with a nice lot of friends."

"Further protest seemed ungracious, so the visitor yielded. Hour after hour passed by, and it was midnight before the visitor could induce his host, who was beginning to feel the effects of a night's drinking and revelry, to accompany him to his home.

"In the morning the host, who evidently felt that nothing had transpired at the clubrooms that could be objected to, asked his friend, 'Well, what is your opinion of our clubroom accommodations?'"

"The rooms are very nicely furnished," was the rather evasive reply.

"But what I want to know is, how did you enjoy yourself in them?"

"As further evasion was useless, the guest said: 'You are asking me a plain question, and I will answer it frankly. I am a single man, and expect soon to get married. If I continue to prosper, I intend to settle down in a comfortable home, and spend my evenings with my wife and my children. As for your clubrooms, if I wanted to neglect my family and my business, and perhaps go to ruin, I think I could soon bring about that result by spending my evenings in your clubrooms; and I am more resolved than ever that when I am once married my home shall be my clubhouse.'"

Now, we would not seem to indicate that the

only proper place for the husband is in the house—that he should not go out in the evening for diversion, social fellowship, or recreation. Not at all. These things are often necessary for his health, his happiness and his well-being. But are they not as essential to the health, the happiness and well-being of the wife as of the husband? If he seeks diversion in the evenings, let it be where his wife may accompany him, and share whatever benefits he enjoys. If family duties or the care of children render it impossible for both to leave home at the same time, then manifestly it is the duty of the husband to divide the advantages and disadvantages with the wife; and if the husband has the true father-spirit, the privilege of frequently remaining at home to spend the evening with his children will afford more pleasure and more profit than could be secured elsewhere.

The husband should plan and arrange to give his wife a proper amount of relaxation and diversion. The limitations of her restricted life make recreation and relaxation essential to the maintenance of good health and a cheerful disposition. But, in all your planning and arrangements, remember that relaxation and diversion may be secured within the home as well as without, and can be there enjoyed by the children also, and by others who may chance to share the home with you. If you and your wife have true father-love and mother-love, you will prefer home and the companionship of your children to any other place, and to the company of any other person or persons. Faithful husbands and wives and well-poised parents will need no specific directions in these matters. They will know how to care for their children, and at the same time not sacrifice health and cheeriness.

These are important subjects for the thoughtful consideration of young husbands, and older ones also ; and while upon this matter, it may be well for those of us who are too apt to delegate to the wife the whole duty of making the home cheery and happy, to read and think upon the following from the pen of Dr. Isaac Farrar:

"How do you go home to your wife after business hours ? Do you not frequently find a tired woman, who has been so hard at work all day with the care of three or four babies, and an incompetent hired girl, that she has found no time to make an afternoon toilet, to meet you as you would like to have her on your return ? Try and be a sympathizing husband now ; embrace your faithful wife and say to her: 'Never mind, my dear, I'm home early to-night. Come now, go and rest yourself, while I put little Clarence and Addie to bed, and if Frank comes in for his supper I will tell Bridget what to get for him.'

"Are you mindful of draughts and slamming doors while she takes her rest for an hour or so, and can you not induce her to take that rest every day ? Remember her days are long, just as busy, and more full of petty cares than yours. A woman is required to be everything, from a reception committee to receive calls in the parlor, to a nurse in the nursery and a chief executive in the kitchen; while a business man devotes himself to a single trade or profession.

"When you undertake to entertain your wife the evenings you are at home, do not have too much to say about the 'scarcity of money;' for perhaps, in her particular case, she knows as much about that as you do; and if the wood and coal bills are larger every year, remember that your family is larger as well; and do not tell her the general dislike you have for children unless they are angels, for they cannot quite be angels during their stay here on earth.

"When the children are in bed and the house quiet, do not seat yourself in the easy chair and read the newspaper to yourself, from editorials to market reports, as if it contained nothing that would interest an intelligent woman. Newspapers read in selfish solitude by thoughtless husbands have made the 'rift within the lute' in more than one happy home.

"How many anecdotes and stories do you tell your wife to provoke a smile or a laugh? How many roses or pinks do you pin on your coat, and how many do you bring home to her? Are you careful of your own appearance in the long evenings when there is no other woman but her to be captivated by your manly charms? I am inclined to believe there is more excuse for her, if her dress has not been changed, her hair made tidy, than there is for you, most noble husband! Perhaps you never gave it a thought; but do not excuse your indifference and neglect of fond attentions, for they are just as dear to that careworn wife of yours at forty-five, or even fifty, years as at twenty-two, when you promised her that you would be true and faithful to her through life's journey. Have you honorably kept your word?

"Your answer may be: 'My wife knows I love her, and that's enough.' She may know it, but it is a pleasant thing to be assured of now and then, and if there were more everyday assurances there would be fewer careless, heart-starved wives."

It is the nature of all women to love to be wooed and won, and after marriage the same nature craves attention, tenderness, and the expression of appreciation, affection and love. No man, even if he were so sordid and selfish as to be moved by no less base or no more worthy motive than the satisfaction of his own sensual nature and consideration for his own personal comfort, could afford to withhold the expression of at least some measure of thoughtful consideration and attention. But any home in which such feelings have to be feigned, because they cannot truly be felt, is one in which commiseration and pity need to have a large place.

Should you ever note upon the part of your own wife the slightest manifestation of indifference and estrangement, put away from your lips, and even from your heart, all words of reproof and reproach, and try again the methods that enabled you to win the affections' of your wife months and years ago. We grant you that there are some women who are regular Xantippes, whom no philosopher can manage, of whom we have given illustrious examples in the lives of some eminent men in the preceding volume, but let us hope that they are not numerous.

There are men, and not a few of them, we fear, who are doomed to disappointment in marriage. It does not take them long to discover the discrepancy between what they thought marriage to be and what it really is. They soon regard this union a mistake, and in a few years, and some even in a few months, denounce marriage as a failure. The truth is that the sole and only failure is found in the mistaken and unworthy views held, concerning marriage, by one or both parties to the contract. Marriage is no failure, but these men are themselves the failures. They belong to a class who hold most degraded views concerning woman and her relation to her husband in marriage. They regard woman as having been created solely to gratify the unbridled lust of man. They married with the idea that in such a union the grossest lust would have the sanction of law, and that in the marriage ceremony the wife relinquished all right to her own body, and for the satisfaction of wearing the white veil and carrying a bouquet of flowers consented to surrender to him not only her rights, but her sense of decency as well. These men who stare decency out of countenance upon the street, who lay traps for the ruin of innocent and unsuspecting girls, who invade the sanctity of home, and whose course through life is like the slimy trail of a venomous serpent, are unfit for marriage—they are unfit to be regarded even as men. No man, it matters not how full his bank account or how fine his clothes, if he holds these low views of woman and of the wife's place in the marriage relation, is worthy of a wife, for he dishonors his own mother and sisters, dishonors every right-thinking man, and his Maker as well. Any man who has in him the seeds of such unworthy sentiments may be sure that even though they may be hidden during the earlier years, they will soon grow, and hasten to a harvest of terrible fruitage.

The happiness of many homes is wrecked in the early struggle to determine whether the will of the wife or the will of the husband shall have pre-eminence. We have even heard brides boasting that in trivial matters they contended with their husbands in order to teach them from the very beginning that they did not propose to recognize any superior right in the husband to direct, or, as they said, "to boss it over them." Brides often object to the word "obey" in the marriage service, and instead of using the words "Love, honor and obey," the substitution is often made of "Love, honor and cherish," or "reverence." If the word "obey" is understood by the husband to mean imperious domination, then it had better be universally expunged. Yet, nevertheless, there is a great deal of truth in the declaration of Napoleon that he would rather have his army in command of one poor general than of two good ones. The careful execution of an ordinary plan is much better than that which comes as the result of divergent views and conflicting opinions.

In an address delivered before the First National Congress of Mothers held in Washington, Hamilton Cushing, the chief of the Ethnological Department of the Government, gave a very interesting account of the custom among the Zuni Indians, who recognize the pre-eminence of the female in everything. The men are not even allowed to hold or to have any right in property, other than through their wives, mothers or sisters. In many marriage unions the wife is easily the intellectual superior of her husband, but the universal custom among civilized nations is to recognize the husband as the head of the house. This is the Christian idea, and the plain teaching of Scripture; not, however, in that mistaken sense which is so often intended when the words are quoted: "The husband is the head of the wife." The Scriptures nowhere justify a husband in assuming imperious domination over his wife. He is "the head of the wife," but in that loving, considerate sense "even as Christ is the head of the Church." The Scriptural teaching is so important and so beautiful that we insert here, in their entirety, two of the principal selections upon this subject. That which relates to the wife we have printed in italics, and that which relates to the husband we have printed in small capitals. But to understand the relation of these two co-ordinate truths, it is necessary that the reader should note carefully the entire context. Paul, in the fifth chapter of his letter to the Ephesians, from the twenty-second to the thirty-third verse, writes as follows:

"*Wives, submit yourselves unto your own husbands, as unto the Lord. For the husband is the head of the wife, even as Christ is the head of the church: and he is the Saviour of the body. Therefore as the church is subject unto Christ, so let the wives be to their own husbands in everything.* HUSBANDS, LOVE YOUR WIVES, EVEN AS CHRIST ALSO LOVED THE CHURCH, AND GAVE HIMSELF FOR IT; that he might sanctify and cleanse it with the washing of water by the word, that he might present it to himself a glorious church, not having spot, or wrinkle, or any such thing; but that it should be holy and without blemish. SO OUGHT MEN TO LOVE THEIR WIVES AS THEIR OWN BODIES. He that loveth his own wife loveth himself. For no man ever yet hated his own flesh; but nourisheth and cherisheth it, even as the Lord the church: for we are members of his body, of his flesh, and of his bones. For this cause shall a man leave his father and mother, and shall be joined unto his wife, and they two shall be one flesh. This is a great mystery: but I speak concerning Christ and the church. Nevertheless, let every one of you in particular SO LOVE HIS WIFE EVEN AS HIMSELF; and the wife see that she reverence her husband."

Here is clearly and beautifully set forth the correct relative pre-eminence in the home. It is the wife recognizing the headship of her husband, as the Church recognizes the headship, leadership and authority of Christ. Upon the part of the husband, his headship is to be exercised in the spirit of that abounding love which led the Son of God to the sacrifice of Himself, both during His life and in His atoning death, for the salvation and blessing of that body of believers who constitute the Christian Church.

The teachings of Peter in his first general letter, or epistle, in the third chapter, from the first to the seventh verse, is as follows:

"Likewise, ye *wives, be in subjection to your own husbands;* that, if any obey not the word, they also may without the word be won by the conversation of the wives; while they behold your chaste conversation coupled with fear. Whose adorning, let it not be that outward adorning of plaiting the hair, and of wearing of gold, or of putting on of apparel; but let it be the hidden man of the heart, in that which is not corruptible, even the ornament of a meek and quiet spirit, which is in the sight of God of great price. For after this manner in the old time the holy women also, who trusted in God, adorned themselves, being in subjection unto their own husbands: even as Sarah obeyed Abraham, calling him lord: whose daughters ye are, as long as ye do well, and are not afraid with any amazement.

"LIKEWISE, YE HUSBANDS, DWELL WITH

them ACCORDING TO KNOWLEDGE, GIVING HONOR UNTO THE WIFE, as unto the weaker vessel, and AS BEING HEIRS TOGETHER OF THE GRACE OF LIFE; that your prayers be not hindered."

Here the teaching is also very beautiful and impressive. The wife is to be in subjection to a considerate and loving Christian husband because it is her privilege and honor; but even though her husband be no Christian, one who "obeys not the Word," still she is to recognize and conform to this teaching, to the end that by her consistent Christian deportment, and that adorning of "the hidden man of the heart" which is to be exhibited in "a meek and quiet spirit" she may win him to a life with Christ.

The husband is to dwell with his wife "according to knowledge," not in ignorance of the peculiar organs and functions of her reproductive nature; for Peter here manifestly refers specially to this, for with wonderful beauty he lifts the marital relation into a holy and sacred light by calling attention to the fact that the husband and the wife are "*heirs together of the grace of life*." In other words, God has taken his power as the Creator of life—think of it! as Creator—and made the husband and the wife joint heirs together of this grace or gift of creative power, which power they call into exercise in the act of reproduction. Surely, intelligence and reverence are essential, both in the husband and in the wife, in order that they may dwell together "according to knowledge."

It would scarcely seem necessary to enjoin industry as an essential to happiness in married life; and yet the happiness of many homes is wrecked on the rocks of ease and idleness. An idle person is like the ship that simply floats upon the seas without a cargo, and without a destination. There are ten thousand directions to shipwreck, but only one course that will bring the mariner to any desired port in safety.

In making labor essential, God conferred a great blessing upon man. The idle man is an unhappy man, and the idle woman is an unhappy woman. Industry is essential to the maintenance of good health, to the proper poise and manly mastery of the sexual nature, to a contented mind, a cheerful disposition, to happiness in the home and spirituality in the life.

Whatever of incentive the past may have lacked, no young husband, unless he is without true manhood, can look into the face of his devoted wife and dependent children without being inspired by the obligation which rests upon him to make adequate provision for every present need and future emergency. His energy, his effort, his wisdom are largely to determine not only the present and future, but also the temporal and eternal destiny of those who gather in dependence about him. Let these be your inspiration. Not all men can amass wealth; nor is this essential. Remember there are many things secured by industry and effort which are more precious than gold. While a competence is desirable, large wealth is seldom a great blessing. There is a world of sound philosophy in the declaration of a very rich man who said: "I worked like a slave until I was forty to make my fortune, and I have been watching it like a detective ever since—for which I have received only my lodging, food and clothes." A noble purpose, seconded by manly endeavor, will secure for your heart and your home what wealth cannot purchase.

We would be alike untrue to your best interests and unfaithful to Him who has called us to the delicate and difficult task we have undertaken in the preparation of these pages did we not say something concerning that which is highest and best in you, and which the Creator designed should dominate over every other department of your nature—namely, the religious or moral nature.

If you want your wife to be happy, do not ask her to struggle onward and upward alone in the Christian life. She will be lonely if the dearest of earthly friends is unwilling to travel heavenward with her. You will double her difficulties if in your life and example you deny the correctness of her precepts and her life. Even if you propose to yourself a life of moral rectitude, yet, to your children, you will become only a stationary guide-board, pointing to their feet the way in which God intended that you should be a living guide. You have not done your duty when you have simply permitted the Saviour to come into your home as the guest of your wife and the Saviour of your children.

He comes to be a guest in your heart, as well as in your home. He comes not only to save your wife and your children, but to save you—to save the father, with the wife and the children.

It is not enough, my dear brother, that you give something now and then toward the support of the church, that you send your children to Sunday-school, that you attend divine service now and then. Your wife and children cannot go to heaven for you. Their lonely struggle is saddened by your absence, and the thought that after having dwelt together with you upon the earth you may be forever separated from them in eternity.

Let me appeal to you as an honest man. What is your duty in this matter? Your duty to your wife, to your children, to yourself, and to your God? If we were to look upon this subject simply in the light of temporal good, all the arguments would be in favor of living a Christian life.

Even if you were to consider this subject on its very lowest plane, you should desire for your wife and your family those larger material blessings which are secured by a religious life. Christians have not only the promise of the life that is to come, but they have the promise also of the life that *now* is. Paul says: "Godliness is profitable unto all things, having the promise of the life that now is, and of that which is to come." We grant you that not every Christian is encumbered with large wealth; neither is every irreligious man plunged into poverty.

While there are here and there instances where ungodly men are possessors of large wealth, these instances are exceptional, and the Scriptural reason not difficult to find. Their riches may be due to the fulfillment of the promise that God will visit blessings upon the children of the righteous from generation to generation. These people may have had praying and God-fearing parents, and on that account the children, in harmony with Scriptural promise, are now being crowned with the consequent blessings. Or, it may be, as the Scripture declares, that the wealth of the wicked is being laid up for the just, and the present wicked possessor may simply be holding this wealth in trust for the righteous descendants who are to come after him. Or, it may be, that God is seeking the salvation of this ungodly individual, for He tells us that "the goodness of the Lord is designed to lead us to repentance."

The actual conditions are not to be determined by taking an exceptional example among the irreligious, but by dividing society as a whole into two classes, and then the result is seen at a glance. In the one class you have the profane, the vicious, the intemperate, the dishonest, the law-breakers, and the defiers of God and man. To this class belongs every man who staggers, reels and falls into the gutter, every tramp who walks the road, and nine-tenths of all the persons who fill our almshouses. It includes, with scarcely an exception, every man and woman who fill our prisons and reformatory institutions; those who crowd the great tenements and live in filth and squalor in the slums of our cities; those whose bodies reek with physical and moral rottenness —these, and many others, constitute the class of the ungodly, and no attentive person can fail to observe that this is the character of that portion which the ungodly have in this world.

Now, turn to the other class. Walk up and down the streets where you find the most comfortable homes, the largest dwellings, the abodes of the most affluent and respectable in any city, and then answer the question, whether or no the wealth of the nation is not to-day largely in the hands of Christian men and Christian women? These are the people who have the best credit, who can draw checks for the largest amounts. Among this class you will find the most influential in business, the owners of our largest mercantile establishments. Men who direct and control the commerce of the world. Men who are at the head of our largest banking institutions, railroad and other corporations. But not only so. These are the people who dwell in the best homes, who eat the best food, who have the largest amount of material comforts. They are the people who enjoy the best health, who have the brightest minds, who produce the best books, the most helpful literature. They have the brightest eyes and the strongest bodies, and when cholera and plague come and sweep away men and women by thousands, it scarcely ever crosses the line which separates these from the intemperate and the vicious, who go down before these scourges like grass before the sickle. Truly, my dear friend, if you are to look at it only from this lowest plane of present good and material comfort, godly living will bring to you the promise of the life that *now* is, and in addition you will also have the promise of the life which is *to come*, a part in the first resurrection, a place at Christ's right hand, and the promise of sitting upon a throne judging the nations—you shall be among those who in triumph enter the eternal city, and receive crowns and robes and palms of victory and eternal rest at God's right hand.

You cannot afford to neglect the spiritual, which is the highest and best of your threefold nature. You should call your entire being into fullest exercise. A Christian is the highest type of manhood, and you owe it to your wife and to your children, as well as to yourself and to your Master, to be satisfied with nothing short of this. If troubled with doubt you will find the difficulty in your own heart. If infidels have filled your mind with misgiving, or suggested unbelief, read "Christianity's Challenge,"* "A Square Talk to Young Men,"† and various other volumes of the Anti-Infidel Library.‡

---

* "Christianity's Challenge," by Rev. Dr. Herrick Johnson, American Tract Society, 269 pages, price $1.00.

† "A Square Talk to Young Men," 94 pages, price 50 cents, by H. L. Hastings, Scriptural Tract Repository, Boston, Mass., 49 Cornhill street.

‡ The Anti-Infidel Library in tract form, 5 cents each, by H. L. Hastings, Scriptural Tract Repository, 49 Cornhill street, Boston, Mass.

CHAPTER V.

THE PHYSICAL COST OF PROCREATION.

BEFORE a ship sails from port with its valuable cargo of goods and its priceless freightage of life, they do what is called "boxing the compass." Naturally the compass would point to the true north, but because of the character of the cargo the needle may be diverted from the true north. To discover whether such local influences exist, they test and correct the compass. The deviation from the true north might be very slight, and in a very short voyage the error might not result in serious consequences, but the interests involved are too momentous to permit of any risk. Before entering upon the new voyage of married life it is essential, for the purity and safety of the two who enter upon it, and also for the well-being of the other lives which may subsequently be added to the family, that the principles by which husband and wife are to be guided should be carefully examined, that errors may be discovered and corrected, for the wrecking of a ship is of less moment than the wrecking of human lives, for these involve not only temporal, but eternal destinies.

The false impressions which young people oftentimes get is due to the general absence of truthfulness upon the part of older and more experienced persons in their conversations upon the subject of the sexual relation. Notwithstanding the fact that the questions which gather about the subjects of sex are of vast moment, yet these subjects have been so little written or spoken about in a pure and reverent way that, for the most part, pure-minded and honest people have banished the subject from the round of ordinary conversation. This abandonment of a sacred subject by the pure and truthful has resulted in the general ignorance and prevailing errors. Among the vile and impure the subject is much talked of, and because of the lack of correct knowledge, statements of the most exaggerated, unreasonable and oftentimes impossible are generally accepted as veritable truth. In dealing both with themselves and others, men are more deceitful and untruthful upon this subject than perhaps upon any other. It is because of these facts that the young and inexperienced so often form the most exaggerated and unreliable opinions upon subjects relating to the relation of the sexes.

That we may the better understand the whole question of the sexual relation it may be well to study the reproductive life of plants and the lower forms of animal life. The knowledge of the lessons they have to teach may prove a profitable subject for thoughtful consideration and lead to valuable conclusions for guidance in the relation between husband and wife.

If with our desire to start with one of the

lowest forms of life we go to the pond and run our finger under the green scum which floats upon its surface, we will find one of the simplest forms of vegetable growth, known as spirogyra. The innumerable threads of green are quite like hairs that lie side by side, in close proximity but not in contact. Under the microscope each of these green threads is composed of long tube-like cells, placed end to end and forming a continuous growth. Under the microscope they very much resemble what in country districts is called bullrushes, or the different sections of a bamboo walking-stick or fishing-rod.

In the spring days, when this growth of green approaches its maturity, it arrives at that mysterious time when the future urgently appeals to it, when each cell feels a strange and irresistible attraction to its neighbor cell. Each reaches out toward the other until a contact is formed, a perfect union is effected, a new germ is created, and the old cells are left lifeless and perish. The union which results in the production of the fertilized seed, in which abides the spirogyra of another springtime, while its beginning costs the life of the parent plant, the verdure that lived in the green scum has passed away, the new germs fall to the bottom of the pond, where, through the drought of summer or the ice and cold of winter, they abide in the sure resurrection of that new life which is to come with the returning springtime.

In the higher forms of life similar illustrations of the great parental sacrifice involved in the act of reproduction are frequently found. This is specially seen among the fishes. During the reproductive weeks life speeds along with great intensity. Under the flow of that larger vitality which greatly quickens and augments certain parts of the organism, the fish increase in size, every part seems to attain its perfection and beauty, and the parent fishes yield themselves to a reproductive impulse that prove fatal to millions of them. After a cod has expelled its million or more of eggs there is not much left of its own body. There is diminished vitality in every part. The male loses his appetite. Great physical changes result. The skin which covers his shrunken body changes in color, his nature becomes irritable and resentful, and he indulges in fierce combats with his fellows.

The fatigue attendant upon the long journeys undertaken by the salmon during the spawning season and the exhausting effects of the fertilizing effort are so great that few survive the trying ordeal. The same results are practically true with regard to the shad. Somewhat analogous changes and results occur with the female, but they are less marked and less destructive. The male is characterized by a more intense activity, while her more quiet nature is her greater safeguard.

The exhaustive and often fatal effects of the reproductive act are very manifest in insect life. Among the insects the reproductive act of the male seems to round out the purpose and complete the period of his life. The exhaustive act is oftentimes speedily followed by death. This same fatal termination is also experienced by the female after she has completed the work of developing and depositing the germ in some place suited for its protection and adapted to its eventual development and growth. In many instances the fertilizing principle is transferred from the body of the male to that of the female during flight, and, strange as it may seem, the intromittent organ of the male and the ovipositor of the female develop and continue only for that brief period which is necessary for the transference of the quickening principle and for the depositing of the egg in a place of safety.

The hive with its hundreds of bees affords an interesting illustration of the subject in hand. The male bee is a drone. His only purpose in life seems to be to await the period when the queen bee in her instinctive desire to perpetuate the life of the swarm is ready to receive the sperm-cells from the male. The drone is stingless and helpless. The germ of the queen bee was developed in a special cell, was fed on royal food and tenderly reared. Her office is not only to preside over the destinies of the swarm, but to her alone is assigned the entire work of reproduction. She never leaves the hive but once, and then upon her nuptial flight, accompanied by a male bee. When the wedding journey is over, and the queen bee has received the sperm from the male, his work is done and his destiny is sealed. Death then ensues either by natural laws, or he is stung to death by the workers, who now regard him as an unnecessary burden upon the gathered stores of the hive.

The queen bee receives the sperm but once, and then, in a mysterious receptacle which Providence has provided, the sperm is stored, and for months, and even for years, for the supply has been known to last for five years, and during this time the millions of eggs which the queen bee lays are each fertilized at will, and, strange to say, her wonderful prolificness does not result in her exhaustion and death, and to prevent this sad result, her hive-mates make it their care that she shall be bountifully nourished with the most sumptuous food.

With the birds, death, as the result of the reproductive act, disappears. The loss which they sustain in reproductive material is comparatively small, yet something of what this costs is manifest by the noticeable changes which take place immediately after they enter upon the mating season. The plumage loses its lustre, the song becomes less frequent and less ecstatic, and the incoming tides of life, which reached their fullness at the period of mating, ebb and recede.

Among the higher forms of animal existence the duration of life is greatly prolonged. The number of the offspring is greatly reduced. The ovum of the female and the sperm of the male become microscopic. The germ of life remains within the body of the mother until it has reached that stage of development which fits it for its independent life in the outer world. The period from conception to birth is greatly prolonged, and the periods of deliverance from the necessity of the reproductive act are alike extended. The higher in the scale the more dependent the offspring, until in the instance of man the offspring is the most helpless and dependent of all. The prolonged dependence of the child upon the care of its parents is calculated to abate the fervor and force of reproductive inclination.

While in man the reproductive act is not the precursor of death, yet it is the premonition of that event and the instinctive effort which nature makes to prevent the extermination of the race.

The inclination to beget descendants is a premonition of the physical dissolution which awaits the individual, and the act itself is always more or less exhaustive to the male, and its results, if too oft repeated, or at periods of brief duration, are disastrous to the female. Notwithstanding these tendencies and results, yet reproduction is the expression of the fullness of physical life and vital force. Its inclination and desire is both normal and necessary, yet it should always be remembered that the increased activity of the reproductive system is secured at the cost of diminished force throughout the remainder of the entire body. No man during the period of the exercise of his reproductive nature is as strong intellectually, physically, or in any other department of his entire being, as during the periods when he is sexually self-contained, or is resting in the calm of sexual repose.

In the lower forms of life the reproductive flame bursts out into one all-consuming conflagration, exhausting to the male and eventually terminating with fatal results to the female. In man this fire burns with a more steady glow, bursting forth occasionally into more intense activity, and then subsiding, but always vitalizing and giving energy to all his powers, and no man can fan this flame into a continuous conflagration without suffering the most ruinous results and disastrous consequences.

Among the lower forms of life the reproductive inclination of the male recurs at those periods when his mate is in the condition necessary to the procreation of the species. After the act of procreation, the sexual passion in both subsides, and the reproductive function is not again called into exercise until after the intervening weeks or months of repose have passed and nature again responds to the necessity of procreation for the purpose of perpetuating the species. Where the periods of ovulation and fecundity recur at brief intervals in the female, the reproductive nature of the male is in a more continuous state of activity, so that a fruitful union may be secured when the reproductive nature of the female is in readiness; but this by no means indicates any physical necessity or reasonable justification for the constant or even frequent exercise of the reproductive function.

Strict continence is not injurious, either to the

unmarried or to the married. Thousands of married men and women are suffering from the effects of excessive sexual indulgence. They drain their physical powers, weaken the intellect, and fail to attain the happiness and grand results which would otherwise be possible to them. All who are familiar with the care of plants know that the best way to preserve their bloom and beauty is to restrain the consummation of the reproductive act. Prevent them from going to seed and the flowers continue to bloom. Remove the anther from the lily and the flower will not fade so soon by several hours. The same is true with the insects. Where they can be prevented from losing their vitalizing sperm they live on beyond the limits of others of their kind who are left free to exercise the privilege of reproduction. An instance is given of a butterfly which continued to live for over two years in a hot-house, while the ordinary period of life to those which exercise the reproductive power complete and end their career in a few short days.

There are times when married people should observe the strictest continence. A state of partial or total intoxication is a just cause for either a husband or wife to deny to the other all marital privileges. Conception at such a time is more than likely to result in the production of idiots or epileptics. The cases on record are too numerous and too well authenticated to admit of doubt in regard to the terrible consequences of conception under such circumstances.

During sickness or convalescence procreation is not only highly injurious to the individual, but at any period before the physical powers have fully regained their most perfect state of health the transmission of life is more than likely to result in the begetting of children who are to be afflicted with mental debility and physical infirmities which shall be so inwrought into the very fibre of their being as to continue through their entire life, utterly beyond the reach of all remedial agents.

We can conceive of no greater wrong that a parent could ignorantly or wilfully inflict upon his unborn offspring than to call them into being at a period when they cannot escape the inheritance of lifelong physical or mental infirmity.

Abstinence from the marital relation in some instances becomes almost absolutely imperative. In the intimate relations of married life the exercise of such self-restraint is not always easy, but it is nevertheless possible. There are well-authenticated instances in the lives of missionaries who have married and immediately gone to climates where conception during the period of acclimation would have resulted fatally who have maintained absolute continence for a period of months and years. We know of an instance where, because of a diseased condition known as vaginismus, the marital relation was attended with such discomfort and pain that for a few years it was only indulged at long intervals, and then totally abandoned, and strict continence maintained for a period of twenty years and more.

Nor is strict continence in married life without illustrations of those who have voluntarily chosen it. There are some married people in this country, more numerous than some suppose, who have adopted the idea of uniform continence, and who call the reproductive nature into exercise for the purpose of procreation only, and who assert that the maintenance of continence secures not only greater strength and better health, but greater happiness also.

CHAPTER VI.

MARITAL MODERATION.

The foundation of marriage and of home can only be built permanently upon the abiding nature of love. Like our own being, love has a twofold nature. Its spiritual part is immortal and unchangeable; its physical part is temporary in purpose and continuance, and is liable to perversion and debasement. The physical may even be permitted to overshadow, debase and quite obliterate the spiritual. In its natural unfolding and manifestation love is very much like the plant that is rooted in the earth while it flowers in the sunlight. The earth and the roots in their relation to each other are essential and even indispensable to the production of the flower, and the flower is alike indispensable to the perpetuity of the plant.

So love has its physical and its spiritual nature. Love is rooted in that unconscious law of our nature which God has enacted for the preservation and perpetuity of human life. "Nothing but a spurious delicacy or an ignorance of facts can prevent our full recognition that love looks to marriage, and marriage to offspring, as a natural sequence." While this is its objective purpose, it yet serves other high ends.

In its twofold nature love ennobles its possessor. It makes him responsive to the love of God upon the one hand and to the love of mankind upon the other. It gives purpose and zest to life, brightens the intellect, quickens the imagination, inspires purpose and imparts physical power. It beautifies and glorifies the individual, and makes him worthy of redemption. "When it is pure and true it unites two souls in bonds of happiness which never chafe, and which become stronger as time passes and the passions become chaste and subdued."

But there is a monstrosity that is known by the same name. The proper name of this monster is lust. It imparts neither beauty nor life. It is like the parasite plant which is not naturally rooted in the earth, but entwines itself about the growing beauty of other plant-life, only to suck out the life-currents from the stem which has lifted it out of the dirt into the sunlight, in return for which its only charity is that it spreads its stolen verdure over the death which it has itself created.

The question of the proper relation of husband and wife in marriage is a difficult one. It is worthy of a volume. The various phases of the subject which crowd upon our mind exceed the limits of a brief chapter. We only regret that we are restricted by limitations beyond which we cannot pass at this present time. Suffice it to say that there are three principal theories with regard to the marital relation. Briefly stated they are as follows:

The first theory assumes that unlimited sexual gratification is essential to the comfort and well-being of the male, and that, whether married or unmarried, he is to seek its gratification, whether lawfully or unlawfully, wherever and whenever he can find an opportunity. It is scarcely necessary to say that this theory is not worthy of the consideration of fair-minded and decent people. It is contrary to the laws of nature, to the laws of God, and to the laws of all civilized nations. The theory is conceived and born of lust. It has been fathered and fostered by the delusions of ignorant people. It is the child of lust and the parent of sensuality. It is disproven by experience and is condemned by the best medical authority in this country and throughout the world. For a discussion of this subject and medical testimony we must refer the reader to "What a Young Man Ought to Know," from page 56 to 67.

The second theory is that in married life the reproductive function is not to be exercised except for the purpose of procreation. While this theory is the opposite extreme of the first, yet it differs from the first in that it has some very strong arguments in its favor. While the results of our investigations do not enable us to assert that it is the true theory, we are yet prepared to say that it is worthy of thoughtful consideration. If it is possible for married people to maintain absolute continence for a period of six months or a year, it must be conceded that it would be possible to extend that time to a longer period. The maintenance of this theory would require such a degree of self-denial and self-control as is far beyond the possession of the great mass of humanity. We fear, also, that there are but few, even if they entered upon a life union with such thought and intention, who would be able to maintain their principles for any considerable period.

The third theory, and that which many men and women who are eminent for their learning and religious life hold to be the correct theory, is, that while no one has a right to enter upon the marriage relation with the fixed purpose of evading the duty of parenthood, yet that procreation is not the only high and holy purpose which God has had in view in establishing the marriage relation, but that the act of sexual congress may be indulged in between husband and wife for the purpose of expressing their mutual affection, augmenting their personal endearments, and for quickening those affections and tender feelings which are calculated to render home the place of blessing and good which God intended.

It is held by those who advocate this theory that while it would be possible to restrict the exercise of the reproductive functions to the single purpose of procreation, yet in the great majority of instances the effort to live by that theory would generally result in marital unhappiness.

It cannot be successfully denied that the perpetuity of the race is the great purpose which God has had in view in instituting marriage.

Procreation and the raising up of a family of children cannot under ordinary circumstances be ignored or evaded without serious physical, intellectual, moral and social results. But neither are mutual love, affection, comfort, consolation and support to be ignored without disastrous results. Due regard is not only to be paid to the perpetuity of the race, but to the well-being and perpetuity of the individual. In his book on the Ethics of Marriage Dr. H. F. Pomeroy says: "Physiologically considered, there can be but one end in marriage—the breeding and rearing of a family; but there are various means which conduce to this end by preserving the mental and physical tone and balance of husband and wife, and cultivating in them a union of regard and affection, without which any mere outward union can be but a travesty of marriage. How far it may be proper to exercise the secondary object of marriage it is impossible to state in any general rule, because individual cases vary so greatly; but it is safe to say that the phase of marriage which is so closely allied to its primary object has an important bearing on the health, happiness and harmony of husband and wife, and so may properly be exercised by those who have a proper regard for the primary end of marriage, even when its relation to this end be but indirect, provided such exercise of it be kept within bounds of mental and physical health."

Personally we are strongly inclined to the acceptance of this third theory. But it must be granted that the acceptance of this theory is attended with many considerations which have their serious perplexities. Perhaps the most constant and most serious difficulty is the question involved in the danger of too frequent conception. To regulate this matter many persons resort to criminal methods, which are nothing short of murder: many resort to expedients which are often unsatisfactory in their result and also ruinous to the health or well-being of either the husband or wife, or both, while others adopt less disastrous but equally unsatisfactory and unreliable measures. Some of these methods are criminal, others are injurious, still others uncertain, and all alike unsatisfactory.

Desirable as it might be to enter upon a full discussion of the various questions involved in the consideration of this phase of the subject, yet because of the general prevalence of vicious living and impure thinking we deem it best not to enter upon a discussion which might effect more evil in some pure-minded persons, by suggestion, than it could accomplish in the reforming of the evil practices of the vicious, and we therefore pass this phase of the subject in silence.

The greatest happiness in married life can never be obtained except by the observance of marital moderation. Just what is moderation in the exercise of the reproductive function in married life it would be very difficult to determine and define. What might be moderation for one man, or for one woman, might be the most extravagant excess for another. The husband may feel inclined to grant himself such indulgence as would entitle him to be regarded as considerate and as within the bounds of moderation when considered in relation to himself personally, and yet the privileges which he grants himself might be most immoderate and most ruinous for his wife; or in some instances the reverse might be the case—indulgence which might be moderate for his wife might be most excessive for him. No husband or wife can determine what is moderation in their own personal instance until they have duly considered the obligation which they are under to the other, and the effect of the relation, not simply upon himself or herself, but upon the other as well. The principle which must govern every husband or wife who desires to be moderate in the marital relation, is, not to seek to grant themselves the utmost indulgence which will enable them to abide within the limits of individual safety only, but so persistently to exercise the spirit of self-control and self-mastery, that they may attain to those best results which are only possible to those who do not call the reproductive function into exercise at too frequent intervals. No man or woman who exercises the reproductive function upon the return of every slight inclination can realize that greatest pleasure and satisfaction which are always possible, but so seldom experienced. The wise husband and the wise wife will not seek that utmost indulgence which brings them to the limit of endurance, but will constantly desire to be governed by such restraint and moderation as will secure for them the most blessed results. To say nothing of morality, intelligence and culture have their province in the exercise of the privileges which are possible to married people. The reproductive sense, like the sense of hunger, or any other sense, is to be brought under the dominion of intelligence and refinement. In the government of our other senses there are laws which no intelligent man will be willing to violate. He will not eat the first food upon which he chances to come, simply because he is hungry. He requires that it shall be of the proper kind, and properly prepared. The worm will seize upon its food regardless of its character, and without any reference to other considerations than that of satisfying its own inclination. Wild beasts will contend over a bone, but man is lifted by intelligence to a higher realm. His food must be of a proper kind, it must be properly prepared, and is to be eaten at appointed intervals. He will not eat that which belongs to another. He desires his food served with proper regard to cleanliness and esthetic taste. He beautifies his table, makes his eating the occasion of social fellowship, takes into consideration the wants and needs of others. If we thus regulate the appetite, why should we not, as intelligent beings, regulate the exercise of the reproductive sense? Why should we yield, like animals, to the first inclination? Why should we despoil ourselves or our companion of the God-given sense of modesty? Why should we be willing to indulge ourselves to such an extent as to injure the one individual whom we love and prize above all others upon earth? Let reason, refinement and the moral sense have their proper sway in the exercise of the reproductive function and the sexual instinct, the same as in the exercise of our other senses.

In a chapter entitled "Rules for Married Persons; or, Matrimonial Chastity," Jeremy Taylor gives the following advice: "In their permissions and license the husband and wife must be sure to observe the order of nature and the ends of God. He is an ill husband that uses his wife as a man treats a harlot, having no other end but pleasure. Concerning which our best rule is that although in this, as in eating and drinking, there is an appetite to be satisfied, which cannot be done without pleasing that desire; yet, since that desire and satisfaction were intended by nature for other ends, they should never be separated from those ends, but always be joined with all or one of these ends: with the desire for children; to avoid fornication; or to lighten and ease the cares and sadness of household affairs; or to endear each other; but never with a purpose, either in act or desire, to separate the sensuality from these ends which hallow it."

It is well also to know what the women have to say upon this subject. Mrs. E. B. Duffey, in her excellent little book, entitled "What Women Should Know," says: "One is often led to wonder if a large class of men are not simply brutes, in all that concerns the physical relations of marriage. Women do not readily make confidential complaints to other women against their husbands. So that when a word —an incomplete sentence smothered before it is fully uttered—is spoken, it must be wrung from the lips by extreme marital brutality. That many women so suffer at the hands of husbands, brutal in this respect, though kind in all others, does not admit of doubt. Disinclination, weariness, ill health, none of these things will excuse a woman from participation in the marital act when her husband's inclinations lead him to require it of her. Strange that, while the law recognizes rape as a crime punishable by severe penalties, there is no recognition whatever of a married woman's right to a control over her own person. I do not know that the most brutal conduct in this respect, if there was no other reason for complaint, would be considered by the courts as a sufficient cause for divorce. Yet any one can readily imagine that it is possible for a man of strong sensual nature, who places no curb upon his appetite, to render the life of the delicate, pure-minded woman, intolerable to the last degree. As mutual affection is the heavenly bond of marriage, so mutual pleasure should also sanction its earthly bond. Love should be prepared to give as well as to receive—to be self-denying when self-denial is required of it. I cannot believe that a wife who sees her husband thus considerate will be unreasonable in her refusal."

But the anxious and honest inquirer still asks, How often may I indulge myself? No general answer can be given to this question. Due reference must always be had to the individual who asks it, and wise counsel would not be possible unless every consideration of the physical condition and health of the wife were allowed their proper place in the solution of the question. What might be moderation for one might be the most destructive excess for another. Some men are strong, have great powers of endurance, and do not know that they have a nerve in their body. Others are very delicate, nervous and dyspeptic. Some physicians are inclined to limit the relation to once a month; upon the other hand, all who have given attention to this subject have learned of instances of excess which do not fall at all short of conjugal debauchery. It might be said that no man of average health, physical power and intellectual acumen can exceed the bounds of once a week without at least being in danger of having entered upon a life of excess both for himself and for his wife.

Each young husband must determine for himself and his wife when they have reached the limit of moderation, and their greatest happiness, physically, intellectually and maritally, will be secured when they have erred upon the side of moderation rather than upon the side of excess. Do not wait until you have the pronounced effects of backache, lassitude, giddiness, dimness of sight, noises in the ears, numbness of fingers and paralysis. Note your own condition the next day very carefully. If you observe a lack of normal, physical power, a loss of intellectual quickness or mental grip, if you are sensitive and irritable, if you are less kind and considerate of your wife, if you are morose and less companionable, or in any way fall below your best standard of excellence, it would be well for you to think seriously and proceed cautiously.

Nor should your observation and study only have reference to yourself. Note carefully the physical, mental and social condition of your wife the day following. You are not only to be the conservator of your own strength, but her protector as well. When you pass the limit of the greatest safety, either for yourself or your wife, you are likely to sacrifice both safety and happiness. Another says: "Even taking the low and sordid ground of selfishly getting the most out of this life, it is wise to abide by temperance and duty in the marital relation, for thus, and only thus, may we derive the most possible satisfaction from it. We may drink the nectar as we will; nature lets us hold the cup, but she mixes it herself; if we drink too deeply she adds water, then gall, and finally, it may be, deadly poison."

Sexual excess is one of the most destructive forms of intemperance, degrading alike the body, mind and morals. We have heard of men who have called the reproductive organs into very frequent exercise, but they have always been men who were noted for nothing except their passion. Everything they eat and drink seems devoted to the maintenance of their sexual nature. They may have enjoyed intellectual advantages, and some of them may even be enrolled as professional men, but every other faculty is dwarfed and weakened that they may foster and fatten their passions. They are eminent in nothing, save as samples of beastliness. Why allow a single passion, the controlling organ of which lies at the very bottom and lowest part of the brain, to usurp and control the entire man, dominate over every other faculty, and render the physical, intellectual and moral faculties and religious sentiments only attendants and slaves!

No thoughtful or considerate husband can afford to disrespect the wishes of his wife. He should reverently consider her inclination as well as his own desire. Throughout the entire range of animal life the condition and inclination of the female fixes and determines the approaches of her mate. Woman is the only female whose condition is disregarded, whose wishes are ignored, whose rights are trampled under foot, and sometimes even denied any right over her own body. Where a woman is in health, and is the loving, devoted wife which she should be, there is not much danger that she will be too strict with the idol of her heart. And, save in exceptional cases, there is but little danger that the wife will be too lenient with her husband. If the wrongs which wives suffer because of the unbridled passions of inconsiderate husbands were publicly known, every virtuous and pure-minded man and woman would be inclined to take up arms for the mitigation of woman's wrongs, and the liberation of this great army of slaves who suffer in silence the servitude from which they have no hope of deliverance except by death.

If you wish to attain your greatest usefulness in life, avoid the undue use of foods which are calculated to stimulate the reproductive nature. Use eggs and oysters, pepper and condiments with reasonable moderation. Do not simulate impure thinking by theatre-going, the reading of salacious books, participation in the round dance, the presence of nude statuary and suggestive pictures; avoid such bodily exposure and postures as mar the modesty of both man and woman; keep reasonable and regular hours, and remember that all these things tend only to enervate and exhaust your wife and to rob and wrong you of the best there is in store for you.

Marital moderation is most easily secured and maintained where married persons occupy separate beds; and, indeed, in many instances such conditions exist as render separate rooms not only desirable, but essential. Mrs. E. B. Duffey, a good and reliable authority on this and related subjects, says: "If the husband cannot properly control his amorous propensities they had better by all means occupy separate beds and different apartments, with a lock on the communicating door, the key in the wife's possession."

Dr. Dio Lewis, in his book entitled "Chastity," when writing of the excesses which lead to estrangement in married life, says: "A very large part of this wretchedness and perilous excess is the natural result of our system of sleeping in the same bed. It is the most ingenious of all possible devices to stimulate and inflame the carnal passion. No bed is large enough for two persons. If brides only knew the great risk they run of losing the most precious of all earthly possessions—the love of their husbands—they would struggle as resolutely to secure extreme temperance after marriage as they do to maintain complete abstinence before the ceremony. The best means to this end is the separate bed."

Many persons recognize the injurious effects which result from two persons sleeping in the same bed, but generally they fear that if they were to occupy adjoining apartments, or even separate beds in the same room, it might lead to local gossip or the suspicion of a lack of harmony or affection. But without informing the patient of the purpose, physicians oftentimes advise a period of absence, either for the husband or for the wife, in order to secure the beneficial result which could be had in their own homes if they would only consent to sleep apart.

Where either the husband or the wife suffers from excessive amative propensities upon the part of the other, great benefit would be derived from avoiding the sexual excitement which comes daily by the twice-repeated exposure of undressing and dressing in each other's presence, and being in close bodily contact for a period of one-third of the hours of each day, for four months in a year, and for twenty years to those who have lived together for a period of sixty years.

There are also the questions of adequate ventilation, the absorption of the exhalations of each other's bodies, the weaker being injured by the fact that the stronger is likely to absorb vital and nervous force, and also the equalization of magnetic elements, which, when diverse in quantity and quality, augment physical attraction and personal affection. Where there is a disparity of physical condition, or a considerable difference of age, or either person is suffering from the effects of any disease which contaminates the atmosphere, separate beds, and oftentimes separate apartments, are essential.

Physical culture is an important matter for consideration in connection with the subject of moderation within the marriage relation. All forms of outdoor recreation which are calculated to produce the best physical condition—dumb-bells, Indian-clubs, exercises of various kinds, frequent bathing, followed by vigorous rubbing of the external surface of the body—are matters of great importance in this connection. If the thought is permitted to centre upon the sexual relation the blood will be diverted from the brain and the muscles, and the entire man will suffer because of the depletion and drain which comes as an inevitable result. Let the thought be turned to other considerations, and by exercise send the blood into all parts of the body, and let the vigorous rubbing after the bath produce a healthy glow, and contribute to good health and to the attainment and maintenance of a well-rounded manhood.

Not only is physical culture essential for the husband, but it is equally important for the wife, who is even more likely to underestimate its value and neglect it altogether, unless she is encouraged to physical effort and bodily exercise by the husband.

Remember that you and your wife owe it not only to yourselves in securing present happiness, but owe it also to your children and to your own future good that you shall possess the best physical results which are possible to you; for what you are, that your children will become after you. If they inherit either physical or mental weakness, the parents who are to care for them will be compelled to pay for their own sad mistakes in vigils and self-denials from which they could have delivered themselves by timely forethought and sufficient care.

The proper mastery of your sexual nature will be worth all it costs. A strong sexual nature is not a curse, but a blessing. God made no mistake in making man what he is; but he never intended that the lower nature should rule over the higher and better nature of man. The struggle is worth all it costs, and the man who gains the mastery grows more manly, more noble, while the man who is overcome becomes less manly, and if lust be given the sway he becomes increasingly beastly.

If you gain and keep the mastery, the struggle will not be endless. With that modified manhood which comes with the hush of the reproductive nature at about middle life, there will come a growing peacefulness and manly poise which will be marked by an increasing strength of intellectual and moral power which will make possible to you in the closing years of your life acquisitions and achievements which were quite impossible in the earlier years.

CHAPTER VII.

DEFECTS AND DEFICIENCIES.

The approach to new relations and untried conditions often awakens in the minds of the unmarried apprehensions which are entitled at least to a brief consideration at this place.

Many young men who are looking forward to marriage spend months of anxious forethought lest there should exist in them some physical incapacity which might unfit them for the new relation into which they are about to enter. Such fears, in the vast majority of cases, are wholly groundless, and in the exceptional instances the insufficiency is generally more seeming than real. Where the previous life has been correct and virtuous there is not more than one case in a thousand where any serious embarrassment may reasonably be expected to arise.

Because of a lack of nourishing food, the neglect of exercise and physical culture, excessive overwork, dissipation and late hours, many young men suffer from sexual weakness and become apprehensive of impotence, and when they contemplate marriage resort to stimulants, or the most foolish expedients, for regaining or testing their sexual power. No more foolish or destructive course could be pursued. The right thing to do is to inquire into the influences which have produced the debility, remove the cause, resort to such indoor and out-of-door exercises as will tend to the best development of the physical man, restore health, increase the ordinary powers of endurance, and then the apprehensions will all disappear.

Physical weakness and general debility, when emphasized by the nervous strain of the ordinary marriage occasion and followed by the excitement inseparable from the earliest marital relation, often result in premature sexual loss and temporary departure of erectile power, and beget apprehension, and even awaken fear.

But even where such instances do occur, they are usually only temporary. Actual impotence during a period of manhood is very rare. Where there is ground for just apprehension the young man should always consult an intelligent and conscientious physician. If he suggests either stimulants or association with dissolute women in order to test your powers, in order to strengthen the reproductive system, accept this as a sufficient evidence of his incompetency, and immorality as well, and betake yourself to another physician. The world has passed on to that period when a practitioner who is so ignorant as to give such dangerous and destructive advice is unworthy of the confidence of the people upon whose credulity and purses he preys, and also of the respect of decent people, or a place among intelligent physicians.

Any young man who has several months remaining before marriage can easily remove all groundless apprehensions by such a full observance of the laws of health, due exercise in the open air, the use of dumb-bells, Indian-clubs and home Exercisers as will develop his physical powers and enable him to come to a just apprehension of his real condition.

Nor need a young man who has selected a bride in good health and in appropriate physical proportions to himself feel any anxieties concerning the deficiencies or deformities in her. Medical authorities affirm that the obstacles to the consummation of marriage are far less frequent in females than in males. The greatest barriers to a proper entrance upon marriage upon the part of men are found in excessive solitary and social vice, and especially in the results which attend and follow venereal diseases, all of which exert a debilitating effect upon the masculine function.

Where a young husband will carefully observe the suggestions made in a later chapter concerning the treatment of his bride, especially from the first day they are married, he will successfully pass any dangers, none of which are likely to appear in the subsequent weeks or years. But where these suggestions are ignored he may be guilty of doing such violence to the sense of propriety of the bride, or so injure her physically, as to make himself the heir of greatest unhappiness for the remainder of his married life. His thought should not only be concerning himself, but especially concerning the deliverance of his bride from a life of invalidism and wretchedness. It seems to us that no wrong which one might do in his ignorance could bring greater remorse and regret than the knowledge of the fact that, without knowing it, he had destroyed both the health and the happiness of one who otherwise would have been a joy and blessing throughout his entire life.

In medical books designed for the profession much space is properly given to the consideration of defects, deformities and monstrosities; but in a book like this, designed to meet the needs of the ordinary individual, such rare and exceptional instances need not be included. Marked abnormal conditions are not often seen in the practice of an ordinary physician, and it is therefore wrong to yield to the tendency to arouse unnecessary apprehensions which can serve no useful purpose, but which often do result in injury to the reader.

Where there exists sufficient evidence of any serious difficulty, or physical incapacity, the young man should not fail to consult an experienced physician of known honor and Christian integrity. Such a man will not betray your confidence, and will be able to afford any necessary relief, and to give judicious counsel and timely assistance. Never, under any circumstances, apply to the quack, the shark or the charlatan, whose only purpose will be to frighten and alarm in order that they may the more successfully extort money from the uninformed, in return for which they can expect nothing better than impoverishment and humiliation, instead of wise counsel and skillful treatment.

But we must at this point speak of the kindred subject of the apprehensions which expectant young husbands often feel with reference to the qualification of the intended bride. As we have already said, deformities and actual incapacity are less frequent among women than among men. Women who know themselves to be suffering from falling of the womb, or other serious womb trouble, should not contemplate marriage. By becoming a wife a woman with serious womb trouble only aggravates her condition, renders herself and her husband miserable—does the very thing which will retard her recovery, and is even in danger of rendering herself wholly incurable. Women who know themselves to be suffering from such ills and ailments should always seek competent medical assistance, cut their corset-strings, devote themselves faithfully to physical culture, and defer their marriage until they have restored these parts to a state of health.

Where either married or unmarried women suffer from female weakness they are generally loath to seek competent medical relief. We have known of married women who have suffered for many years the results of injuries received during confinement who could easily have been not only relieved, but permanently cured, had they applied to a competent physician, disclosed their real condition, and submitted to intelligent treatment.

The same is true of young, married people. Where any slight incapacity or obstacle is found in their new relation they should promptly seek some competent medical advisers, and not permit weeks to elapse, until, on account of their neglect, that which could easily have been remedied in the beginning has become the source of embarrassment, estrangement, or, possibly, some permanent nervous affection. Where it is the wife who needs medical attention, her modest nature may cause her to shrink from examination or counsel, but when she remembers that medical specialists are constantly consulted upon kindred subjects there should be no hesitation in seeking their counsel and assistance. The utmost frankness on the part of the patient should always enable the physician intelligently to understand her condition, while that native female modesty which is the attestation of her virtue will be both her adornment and her defense.

With the increasing number of well-equipped doctors, intending brides in increasing numbers are wisely seeking such counsel as will assure them that there exists no impediment to the formation of a happy marriage. Were this course universally followed it would remove much mental anxiety, possible perplexity, and even marital infelicity. It would disclose to those who have serious womb trouble their unfitness to become wives and mothers, and thus enable the unfortunate ones to escape the unhappiness and misery which marriage is sure to bring both to them and to their husbands. It is always infinitely better to know the facts before it is too late to escape the wretchedness which the marital relation is sure to entail; and then, where no infirmities or barriers exist, the knowledge of that fact will bring an assurance which will be worth many times the embarrassment and expense involved. This is the legitimate, reliable and proper way for every intending bride to secure such information, and the only way to which a virtuous and pure-minded woman could yield her consent.

CHAPTER VIII.

PURITY AND FIDELITY.

The happiness of the individual and of the family often depends upon the influence and effects of very plain and everyday considerations, and in closing Part First there are a few things which we desire to impress upon the mind of the young husband which to some may seem unimportant, but which, in fact, are very important, and your failure duly to observe any one of which may result in your home, as it has in thousands of others, in the blighting of happiness, in personal injury, in injustice and wrong to wife and children, and even in the wrecking of the home itself.

See to it that you have a pure breath. You have no right to defile your body, or render your breath impure or offensive in any way, and especially by the use of tobacco and liquor. You have no more right to defile the air which your wife is to breathe than you have to defile the water which she is to drink, or to sprinkle some disagreeable or loathsome substance upon the food which she is to eat; and the magnitude of this wrong would be increased in proportion to the extent to which it adds to her discomfort or injures her health. To say the least, the use of tobacco is a selfish habit, and if you desire to be just and equal, you should be willing to apportion to your wife for some personal gratification of her own an amount equal to the money which you daily or annually expend upon yourself for the use of tobacco. The tobacco habit is an expensive one. It not only costs an expenditure of a large amount of money annually, but results almost universally in nervousness and irritability. If you use tobacco in any form and will observe yourself closely, noting the difference between the periods when you omit its use and when, upon the other hand, you do not use it, you will be convinced that it tends very perceptibly to render you sensitive, irritable and uncompanionable. But this is not all. It so permeates your entire being as seriously to affect the children which you beget and bring into the world.

No man, we care not how indifferent he may be to the effect upon himself or to the comfort of his wife, can be so insensible to the effect of his own life in determining the character, happiness and destiny of his children, as to be indifferent to the consideration of the results of the use of tobacco upon his descendants. You may often have noticed that men and women of good physique, and apparently enjoying the best of health, become the parents of weak, nervous and sickly children. It would be both unjust and untrue to assert that in every such instance the result could be accurately traced to the use of tobacco, but the evidence that tobacco is the real cause can be established in at least *some* instances. Many a child of inferior physical and intellectual capacity has been defrauded of its larger endowment because the father who begot it was addicted to the use of tobacco. If the teachings of the most reliable medical authority upon this subject are to be accepted, it would be possible to select from any community the finest physical and intellectual specimens of men and women and let them both become addicted to the use of tobacco, and then marry among themselves, and in a single generation or two their descendants would fall far below the physical and intellectual average of the children of other parents who do not use the weed in any form.

The subject of intemperance we have fully treated in the preceding volumes of this series, and we must refer the reader to them in that place, especially the book addressed to young men. Liquor is not only a curse to the individual who uses it, but it wrecks the health and happiness of the wife and curses their yet unborn children. It not only affects their morals, health and intelligence, but where the children are not born imbeciles or idiots they often inherit the appetite for drink and become depraved and drunken to the third and fourth generation. The great minds which have shone in the intellectual firmament of the past, or brighten and bless the present generation, were not begotten of parents who were given to excess and dissipation. Many a man whose descendants might have been lustrous and happy, owe their enfeebled minds and blighted happiness to the indiscretion and excess of the parents who brought them into the world. When God designed to raise up a Samson he said to the mother: "Thou shalt conceive and bear a son. Now, therefore, beware, I pray thee, and drink not wine, nor strong drink, and eat not any unclean thing, for the child shall be a Nazarite unto God from the womb, and he shall begin to deliver Israel out of the hands of the Philistines." The same laws of heredity exist to-day, and they cannot be ignored without imperiling the health and the happiness of those who are to come after us.

If you love your wife or value your own happiness, let us urge upon you the duty of fidelity. This is a duty that you owe to your wife in the same proportion that she owes fidelity to you. God has made but one standard of integrity and virtue, and this is enjoined alike upon men and women. God says, "Thou shalt not commit adultery." He does not say women shall not, or that men shall not. There is no discrimination between men and women.

The word "thou" means the person who reads or hears—the person addressed, whether male or female, young or old, king or peasant, high or low, learned or unlearned, rich or poor, white or black, bond or free. It is alike binding upon all, without abatement or modification, regardless of sex, race, class or condition, and without reference to time, place or circumstance.

What is true of this commandment is also rue of them all. God has not made one set of laws for men and another for women. Neither does He excuse or condone in men what He condemns in women. He holds both alike answerable to the same unerring standards of social and moral purity. Whatever may be the attitude of those who entertain lax moral views, society has no right to condone in man what it condemns in woman. What is wrong for her is wrong for him, and infidelity or unfaithfulness is a crime in either.

In addition to the moral wrong there is also the great physical risk. The unmarried man who leads a life of vice, to some extent, at least, only imperils himself; but the married man imperils his wife and his children in addition. The most reputable physicians can bear ample testimony to the frequency that women apply to them for relief from aches and ills suffered by themselves and their children, the nature and source of which these wives do not suspect, and the terrible and ineradicable nature of which they are totally ignorant. Such is the terrible punishment inflicted by guilty husbands and fathers upon their innocent and unsuspecting wives and children. Hundreds of cases might be named; but let us give a single illustration, narrated to us by one of the most eminent physicians of this country, whose name and residence are not essential, as somewhat similar instances come frequently to the attention of physicians.

A young man of a wealthy family, who had been a couple of times treated for gonorrhœa, married a beautiful bride in a prominent and wealthy family. A couple of weeks after his marriage he came to the physician with one of those small sores called a chancre, which is the unmistakable evidence of the presence of syphilis. Careful investigation disclosed the fact that at the time of his marriage he had a concealed chancre, and which, although unknown to himself, had nevertheless been communicated to his bride. The treatment was prompt and of the most skillful character, but serious results were speedily manifest. The primary sore was followed by its secondary results. Sores appeared upon the different parts of her body, the mucous membrane was affected, and every hair upon the entire person of the wife fell out. She did not have left so much as eyebrows, eyelashes, or even hairs in her nose, and, as in some instances after a serious attack of typhoid fever, months were necessary before the hair started again to grow. When it did grow it returned coarse and wiry, and when about an inch or inch-and-a-half long it very much resembled goat's hair. It could not be combed—nothing could be done with it. She looked like a fright—was an astonishment to her friends and an embarrassment to herself.

With no knowledge of the terrible nature of her disease, it was difficult to induce her to persist through months for a period of at least two years in taking her medicines. At intervals during the years that followed she gave premature birth to children, which, whether born dead, or living for a day or two, were masses of disease and corruption. After four or five of such miscarriages she finally gave birth to a child that at the time of its coming into the world seemed healthy. Not long after the birth of this child the family removed from the community, and the physician was unable to note the effects of the inheritance which no child under such circumstances could possibly escape.

While this case was impressive, it was by no means exceptional. We have learned of instances where persons of unbounded wealth have communicated the syphilis to their wives, and all the skill which wealth could command has not been able to eradicate the disease or deliver the unhappy sufferers from the consequences of the criminal unfaithfulness of the guilty husband.

But there are consequences less manifest to the eye, but no less deadly and destructive in effect, which come to the innocent and unoffending wife as the result of the vice and unfaithfulness of her husband. One of the most eminent physicians of Philadelphia, in conversation with the author, assured us that the effects of gonorrhœa, or clap, which are suffered by the wives is something alarming. Even where the husband has not communicated the disease while it was active in himself, but where the intending husband may have supposed that he was entirely cured of gonorrhœa for a period of two years or more, he may yet communicate the lurking remnants of that disease to the vagina, the effects soon extending up into the womb, out through the Fallopian tubes, oftentimes reaching the ovaries and necessitating their removal, making it necessary to unsex the woman in order to save her from the wretchedness and misery which are inseparable from the death which they so often preface.

An eminent practitioner in New York, when addressing the last annual convention of the State Medical Society, called special attention to the prevalent effects which wives suffer as the result of gonorrhœa contracted by their husbands, and said that a few years ago it was his custom, when women with certain symptoms came to him for consultation, to request a private interview with the husbands in order that he might discover whether past unfaithfulness since marriage or a life of vice prior to marriage was not the cause of the trouble. He said that latterly, however, the best medical authorities were agreed that it was not necessary to subject the husband to this trying inquisition, for the symptoms and conditions which established the correctness of the diagnosis were a sufficient proof of the source of all the wife's troubles. Thousands of husbands who bemoan the fact that their wives are complete physical wrecks are themselves the authors of the ruin which has been wrought.

Nor is this all; fathers have often carried the disease home, and by the use of towels have communicated the virus of the disease to the eyes of their children or some member of the family, from which total blindness has come as the inevitable result. We learned of one instance in which the father communicated the disease to his entire family, including several small children, who took their bath in the same tub, but in different water, after the father had bathed.

For a fuller unfolding of the awful consequences of the diseases which accompany vice we must refer the reader to the book " What a Young Man Ought to Know," from page 93 to 153. All that has there been said in favor of a chaste and pure life can be enjoined with even greater emphasis on those who are married.

But what if a guilty husband and father could escape the dangers of disease, the detection by his wife, and could even escape the lashings of his own guilty conscience, which will smite with sevenfold force as the years advance, yet how terrible for him to remember that transmission is the law of heredity, and that a licentious father is the legitimate predecessor of a vicious child. Is it comforting for a father to anticipate with certainty that all the vices which have corrupted his life, blighted his home and debased his moral nature are to be transmitted to his offspring? How shall he, in the after years, when his own children go wrong, be comforted with the thought that what they are he was, and that what he desires them to be is what he himself should have been. Julia, the daughter of Augustus, was as bad as her father, and gave birth to a child of equally strong propensities. These are the influences which have not only destroyed the happiness of homes, but have wrecked the destinies of nations. By the love you bear your wife, by the love which you have for your children which are and which are to be, by the respect which you have for yourself and the fear that you should have for your God, by all that is sacred in marriage and in home, by all that is to desired in this world and in the world to come, we plead with you, for your present, future and eternal good, that you maintain your marriage vow inviolate.

PART II
CONCERNING HIS WIFE

CHAPTER IX.

THE BRIDE.

WE now come, in Part Second, to consider what a young husband ought to know concerning his wife. In this chapter we desire to speak of what he ought to know of his wife while she is yet a bride. As soon as the minister has pronounced them husband and wife she is as truly the wife as she is later on, and we only use the word "bride" in that commonly accepted sense which refers to the earlier days and weeks of her married life.

We cannot enter upon the thought of this chapter without being conscious of the fact that doubtless thousands of young men will turn to these pages for information concerning the marriage relation who have themselves not yet entered the marriage bond. There is nothing in this book which a young man of mature years may not properly know. Indeed, every young man of mature years ought to possess the information which this volume contains. But we are also conscious of the fact that many young men who are engaged to marry, or are already married, will turn to these pages expecting to find here some means of deliverance from the results of mistakes which, in his lack of knowledge, he has already made. As we enter upon the duty of telling the young husband what he ought to know concerning his bride, we feel the importance of saying that the information which he gathers from these pages will be but partial, unless he has the information concerning woman contained in the preceding volume of this series.

In telling a young husband what he ought to know concerning his bride, it is especially important that he should first understand the nature and purpose of the reproductive organs, the right relation of man to woman, and the correct teachings concerning marriage; and for the unfolding of these subjects we must refer the reader to Chapters VII., VIII. and IX. in "What a Young Man Ought to Know."

In addition to what we have said in Chapter III. of this volume, in reference to the physical, intellectual, moral and sexual differences between men and women, it is necessary now to call the attention of young husbands to the fact that in woman there exists less sexual desire and satisfaction than in man.

Perhaps of the great majority of women it would be true to say that they are largely devoid of sexual pleasure. In regard to the intensity of the sexual instinct, women might with some accuracy be divided into three classes. The first class, which includes the larger number, is generally supposed to be quite devoid of sexual inclination and feeling. The condition of this class may be accounted for in three different ways. In some it is the result of ill health, produced by lack of sufficient exercise and outdoor recreation; because of excessive social demands, late hours, indigestible food, the enervating and exhaustive effects of novel-reading, and especially also of tight lacing, with all of its sad effects in debilitating and displacing the sexual and vital organs which are located in the pelvic and abdominal cavities. If women could but realize what pleasures might be theirs, if they would only live in a rational way, there would be but few men and women left to ask the question whether marriage is a failure.

Another cause of sexual indifference in a large class is found in the fact that some regard the existence of passion in women as derogatory to their sex. There are wives who pride themselves upon their indifference to the conjugal relation. They speak of their coldness and indifference as though it were a virtue, instead of a defect. The fact is, they are simply proud of their deficiency. With this, as with the proper exercise of every other bodily function, God has associated satisfaction and pleasure. The reception of food, which is to sustain and nourish life, is attended with pleasure. Seeing and hearing are attended with pleasure. The exercise of all of our bodily senses is designed to bring us pleasure and a sense of satisfaction. The exercise of the reproductive function is attended with great cost physically, financially, and in every way, and God has meant that to this great sacrifice man shall be prompted by a pleasure which shall be correspondingly great.

God has designed that the act of reproduction should be recognized both as a duty and a pleasure, and the feeling which prompts to the perpetuation of the species is as proper as that which inclines the individual to the preservation of his own life or health. There can be no doubt but that in conception God has assigned an important office to inclination and sensation, for while authorities are agreed that conception may take place without attendant emotion upon the part of the female, yet the result is more assured, and the product of such a union is of a higher standard when both persons participate in the pleasures which invite to its consummation. This sexual indifference upon the part of the wife may sometimes be largely due to the fact that she and her husband are illy mated, physically, morally or socially; or because differences of education and divergence of views have produced that lack of harmony which has, at least measurably, blighted the affections.

There can be but little doubt that much marital indifference upon the part of wives is due to chronic constipation, which is so prevalent among women.

Another cause of this indifference upon the part of some wives, and this is a very small class, is due to malformation, local obstruction, because of an imperfect rupturing of the hymen, or, in rare instances, to a disease known as vaginismus, rendering the act not only devoid of pleasure, but possessed of actual discomfort and suffering. Where these conditions exist, prompt and competent medical assistance is needed for local treatment and judicious advice.

The second class is composed of women who find in the marital relation a moderate and normal pleasure when they are in health, and if indulged in at times which are agreeable to them, and at suitable intervals. This class represents, doubtless, those women who are more normal in this respect than those who belong to either of the other extremes. They constitute the middle class, and probably the largest number.

The third class represents the few in whom sexuality presides as a ruling passion. This class is by no means as numerous as some might imagine, and such women should never be married except to men of good health, strong physique, large powers of endurance, and with a pronounced sexual inclination. When a man with only moderate sexual inclination is united to a woman of this class it is a question which is more to be pitied, the husband whose wife is totally devoid of sexual instinct, or the man whose wife is sexually insatiable. While there are a few women of this class, yet the rule remains that in man the sexual instinct is more pronounced than in woman, and that man constitutes the active and aggressive division of the human family; for while a certain female may possess a more pronounced sexual nature than a certain male, yet in her sexual nature she is not as pronounced as the most active male.

While among all species the male is the more active and aggressive, yet any one who has given attention to the reproductive act among animals will have noticed that in no instance can the male force this relation upon the female without her acquiescence, and in most instances the time of copulation is wholly determined by the condition of the female. It is only when she is in condition to conceive that she will receive the male, and at those periods her condition inspires him to the act. We cannot but believe that this is also intended to be the rule among human beings, although, strange to say, the wishes of the wife are oftentimes wholly ignored, and she submits reluctantly, or is wholly overborne by the exactions of an inconsiderate or brutal husband.

If this subjugation of the wish and the will of the wife to the will of the husband is the result of the curse pronounced upon Eve, "Thy desire shall be to thy husband," the chastisement of woman has been truly severe, for no sorer punishment could well be inflicted than to be deprived of the right of ruling over one's own body, and being placed in subjection to the capricious will and exacting demands of an unreasonable husband. If the wrongs which wives suffer in this respect are the result of the fall of our first parents, we should nevertheless rejoice that now the spiritual and material blessings which have been restored by the Second Adam are also to be shared by woman, and in all the world no other person should be so anxious to crown her with the fullness of her natural rights as the man who will by such an effort vindicate the nobility of his own manhood and secure for himself the largest blessing and happiness, because he is her husband.

Not only is the reproductive nature of woman less pronounced than in man, but its continuance in her is of a much shorter duration. At about forty-five years of age, and in some very much earlier, the reproductive nature of woman undergoes those changes which render conception and childbearing impossible. At that period her sexual nature takes upon itself modifications which are more pronounced than those experienced by the male when a somewhat similar sexual hush comes to him. The character of these changes, and what they involve both to the husband and to the wife, are treated at length in the fourth volume of this series addressed to men at forty-five, and it is well that young husbands should know what the future has in store for them, and so regulate their married life that the later years may bring them the largest possible good and blessing.

The effect of the sexual relation upon newly-married men and women is oftentimes very noticeable. Sometimes those who previously seemed hearty and strong lose their bloom and vigor and become emaciated and miserable. Sometimes the reverse is the case. Especially among women, there are noticeable instances where the family heredity is good, no organic trouble exists, and yet the individual is wholly miserable, and after marriage speedily develops into a strong and hearty woman. There are some who improve somewhat in health, but who avoid parenthood, and thus defraud themselves of the acquisition of perfect health. These cases, however, are rather the exception, and so much is involved in marriage that no man or woman can afford to take such serious risks, because exceptional instances do rarely occur. Yet the fact remains that there are some who are weak and worried and restless before marriage who become hopeful, restful and strong after marriage ; while others, who were well situated and contented in their sphere, accept, in marriage, conditions which result in producing a nervous, despondent and restless disposition.

If the marital relation of these people could be accurately known the cause of these noticeable changes might oftentimes be found in the moderation maintained by the one class and the excessive sexual indulgence the cause in the other. Sexual excess is quite common among married persons. In the husband it results in the destruction of physical power and in the weakening of the intellect as well. Force used in this way is not available for use intellectually, and the consequent effects unfit for study, mental activity, and oftentimes for all kinds of business. It renders the husband nervous, morose, and uncompanionable. The man who is guilty of excess not only destroys his own capacity for pleasure, but is alike unjust to his wife. He renders her incapable of marital pleasure, and also renders her incapable of bringing to him the satisfaction which he seeks. Such a husband destroys the amiability of his wife, renders her weak and nervous, converts her into an invalid, and imposes upon himself large financial outlays for medical advice and attendance. Such a husband deliberately, but not always knowingly, consumes and destroys the physical qualities which made the wife attractive to him, and destroys the very foundation upon which all happiness in the home must rest. Excessive sexual tendencies among men are generally the result of early self-pollution, later illicit relations, reveling in vile stories, nude pictures, the reading of suggestive novels, the polluting of the imagination, and incorrect ideas of the proper relation in marriage. Thought is allowed to dwell too much upon these subjects, the flow of blood to the sexual parts becomes excessive, and the only remedy is by purifying the mind, correcting the ideas, resolutely determining to be moderate and considerate, removing all causes of undue sexual excitement, resorting to the bath, being judicious in the diet, giving due consideration to physical culture, and taking such an amount of exercise daily as is calculated to secure the best physical results and most effectual sexual mastery. The man who needs to be helped in the direction of moderation would do well to confide in his wife that her influence over him may be helpful and corrective, for in this, as in other things, a discreet and considerate wife is her husband's best balance-wheel.

CHAPTER X.

THE CARE OF THE BRIDE.

FEW young husbands are intelligent guardians of their brides. Indeed, when first entering upon the marriage relation, young husbands are in danger of making some very serious mistakes. Many a husband has had cause to regret that in his lack of consideration he has allowed his passion to awaken in his wife such a feeling of disgust as to obliterate her affection for him, to blast the prospects of all future happiness, and render both himself and wife miserable throughout all their subsequent years.

In the first place a young husband should know that many women, even at the time of their marriage, are totally ignorant of all questions relating to sex. There are some women who do not so much as know that there are any physical differences between men and women. There are others who may know there is some difference, but into whose minds the thought of coition has never once entered. While this may not be true in a majority of cases, yet it is true in a large number of instances. We have even known of young wives who have approached the period of their first confinement who did not know the cause of their increasing bodily size; and we recently learned of an instance where the physician was already in the room to attend the expectant mother, who thought that she was to be delivered of her child by a surgical operation. She thought that the doctor was to make an incision in the abdomen, and remove her child in that way.

To say that all this is culpable ignorance does not, however, remove the fact. Young husbands do well to recognize the fact that such ignorance exists, and that, in addition to such possible ignorance upon the part of his own bride, there is that general condition of exhaustion and debility which follows as the result of the weeks of preparation and nervous excitement which have preceded and culminated at the time of the wedding festivities. We have already dwelt upon this phase of the subject, and we need not enlarge upon it here. With the poor it is weeks, and sometimes months, of sewing and preparation. With the rich it is the meeting of social exactions and requirements, formal visitations, and then senseless seclusion. In each instance the results are equally enervating, bringing most brides, whether rich or poor, to the one great event in their lives in an exhausted and nervous condition. To say the least, this uniform physical depletion entitles the bride to the most thoughtful consideration and most gentle treatment that the young husband can exercise.

With ignorance upon the one side, inconsideration and ungovernable passion upon the other, the combination is unfortunate and the results are oftentimes serious. The first act in the drama which is to culminate in separation and an effort to secure a divorce, is often enacted upon the night of the very day which witnessed the marriage ceremony and was attended with the congratulation of friends. The ignorance and inconsiderateness of both are alike to blame for this sad result—the wife for her lack of knowledge and consideration, and the husband for his lack of intelligent and thoughtful appreciation of the delicacies and dangers of his new relation.

In Greece the custom prevails of allowing three days to intervene between the marriage ceremony and the consummation of marriage. It would be well if such a custom prevailed everywhere. It would allow the exhausted, nervous, timid bride to bring to the consummation of the marriage relation renewed vigor and mental composure. It would prepare the mind of the young husband for such self-possession and restraint as would be becoming in this new relation, and would secure for him a happiness greatly heightened in intensity, and that would be prolonged through all the years that lie beyond.

It is enough to make a thoughtful and considerate man blush to think of the scores of wives who annually confess to their physicians that the only rape that was ever committed upon them was by their own husbands the first day of their married life. We recently heard of an instance where the expressed impatience and manifest impetuosity of the young husband, the moment he came into the bridal chamber with his young wife, awakened in her mind such a feeling of disgust that after a brief parleying the young wife left the room and refused ever to return to her husband, and thus terminated abruptly what, with thoughtful and considerate approaches and manifest affection, might have resulted in a union of lifelong happiness.

In his book, entitled "Plain Talks on Avoided Subjects," Dr. Henry L. Guernsey says: "Tenderly and with great consideration should these privileges be accepted, for, contrary to the opinion of many men, there is no sensual passion on the part of the bride that induces her to grant such liberties. Then how exquisitely gentle and how forbearing should be the bridegroom's deportment on such occasions. Sometimes such a shock is administered to her sensibilities that she does not recover from it for years; and in consequence of this shock, rudely or ruthlessly administered, she forms a deeply rooted antipathy against the very act which is the bond and seal of a truly happy married life."

Mrs. E. B. Duffey, in her book entitled "The Relations of the Sexes," says: "Do not be in too great haste to brush the bloom from the fruit you covet. It will lose half its attractions at once. Practice in lawful wedlock the arts of the seducer rather than the violence of the man who commits rape, and you will find the reward of your patience very sweet and lasting. This bud of passion cannot be forced rudely open. Its development must be the work of time. If the young wife is met with violence, if she finds that her husband regards the gratification of his own desires more than her feelings—and if she be worn and wearied with excesses in the early days of her married life, the bud will be blighted. The husband will have only himself to blame if he is bound all his life to an apathetic, irresponsive wife. It is easy to imagine the unsatisfactory conjugal relations which are brought about in punishment of the husband's early impetuosity and ignorance. He finds an unreciprocal wife, doubts her affection for him, because, with his masculine nature, he cannot conceive of a love unblended with passion. She, in her defrauded womanhood, feels aggrieved and debased by any conjugal approach—especially by an enforced one—and finds it equally hard to understand how affection and passion can be united; the one she knows to be so self-forgetful and denying, and the other she has such abundant cause for believing utterly selfish and rapacious."

The excesses which are likely to follow after the earliest experiences of married life are also to be cautiously guarded against. The author whom we have just quoted says: "I will venture to say that there is not one man in fifty who in the first years of his married life is not guilty of sexual abuse towards his wife, which effect is alone sufficient to account for the great prevalence of female diseases. Not that every woman is injured by it to the extent of inflammation and ulceration, yet many are. I am not running a tilt against married men. I blame them for no intentional wrong—only for ignorance. And women are also equally to blame in this matter. They are just as ignorant as their husbands, and often allow themselves to yield to demands or importunities when, if they were to consider it a conscientious duty to refuse, they would do so.

"The tender, delicate organs of generation in women are often abused to such an extent by too frequent use that they become inflamed and ulcerate, and render the woman an invalid. Even the husband does not see the cause or measure the extent of his folly, but persists in his selfish course in spite of the sufferings he causes his wife, constantly aggravating her disorders, and rendering them more and more hopeless of cure. Thus the husband, kind and attentive in all other matters—who would not allow the winds of heaven to visit the cheek of his wife too roughly—becomes, in this one respect, a very—I was about to say brute; but the animal creation presents no parallel case, so I find no appropriate word in comparison."

In his book entitled "The Transmission of Life," Dr. George H. Napheys, in writing upon this subject, says: "The consequence is that in repeated instances the thoughtlessness and precipitancy of the young husband lay the foundation for numerous diseases of the womb and nervous system; for the gratification of a night he forfeits the comfort of years. Let him, at the time when the slow-paced hours have at last brought to him the treasures he has so long been coveting, administer with a frugal hand and with a wise forethought. Let him be considerate, temperate, and self-controlled. He will never regret it if he defer for days the exercise of those privileges which the law now gives him, but which are more than disappointing if seized upon in an arbitrary, coarse, or brutal manner.

"The husband should be aware that while, as a rule, the first conjugal approaches are painful to the new wife, and, therefore, that she only submits and cannot enjoy them. This pain should not be excessively severe, nor should it last for any great length of time—not more than one or two weeks. Should the case be otherwise, then something is wrong, and if rest does not restore the parts a physician should be consulted. It is especially necessary that great moderation be observed at first, an admonition which we the more urgently give because we know it is needed, because those specialists who devote their time to diseases of women are constantly meeting patients who date their months and years of misery from the epoch of marriage."

The pain and inconvenience to which the doctor refers in the preceding paragraph is oftentimes due to the presence in young wives of what is known as the hymen. This is a thin membrane which nature places near the lower extremity of the vaginal passage to protect the delicate linings of the reproductive organs of the female against the admission of any foreign substance, exposure to cold, or any other influence which might tend to the injury of the reproductive nature. With the growth of the body this membrane sometimes acquires such consistency or strength that the rupturing of it is attended with inconvenience, and oftentimes with much pain. This fact alone should render a young husband very considerate, dispassionate, and thoughtful.

The pain attendant upon the rupturing of the hymen is not so much due to the sensitiveness of the membrane itself as the fact that it adheres to the walls of the vagina, and any lateral pressure brought to bear upon the hymen imposes such a tension where the hymen is attached to the walls of the vagina as to produce, in some instances at least, intense pain. The rupturing of the hymen is often attended with a small quantity of blood, sometimes scarcely perceptible, and at other times more considerable.

It was at one time thought that the presence of the hymen was an unmistakable evidence of virginity, and its absence was regarded as a cause for suspicion, if not a proof, of previous sexual relation. While it is true that in most virgins the hymen does exist, yet we do not have the slightest hesitation in saying that it does not exist in all. It may be ruptured and destroyed by a slight accident during childhood, is sometimes even destroyed at birth; in abnormal cases it may need to be destroyed mechanically by the family physician in order to remove it as an impediment in the more easy flow of the monthly period.

Mrs. E. B. Duffey, in "What Women Should Know," when writing of the test of virginity, says: "It is popularly believed that the husband receives proof, upon the consummation of his marriage, of the previous chastity of his wife. If he obtains this evidence it is safe to accept it as conclusive, though rare exceptional cases are to be met with in which the evidence counts for nothing. If, on the other hand, the proof is wanting, it is most unjust and cruel, on the strength of this alone, to charge a wife with want of chastity previous to marriage. It is not uncommon for accidents, which may occur at any time, and which may even date back to birth itself, to destroy this evidence, or it may never have existed."

Dr. Napheys says: "The presence or absence of the hymen is no test. There is, in fact, no sign whatever which allows even an expert positively to say that a woman has or has not suffered the approaches of one of the opposite sex. The true and only test which any man should look for is modesty in demeanor before marriage, absence both of assumed ignorance and a disagreeable familiarity, and a pure and religious frame of mind. Where these are present he need not doubt that he has a faithful and chaste wife."

It is important for young husbands to know that when a serious inconvenience is experienced in the consummation of marriage, if not easily removed by care and consideration, but remains an impediment or a pain for a period of days, or of a couple of weeks, medical advice and assistance should by all means be sought. In the case of women who have advanced in years before marriage such difficulties often occur, and medical assistance is the safest, most sensible and speediest source of delivery.

We cannot pass this point without seeking to impress upon the young husband the danger liable to result from the use of wine and other stimulants upon the occasion of his marriage. One of the most terrible afflictions which can come to any home is the birth of an idiot, and if the statements of medical authority are to be relied upon, the birth of these unfortunate burdens to their parents is due to their conception at a time when either the husband or the wife, or both, were under the effects of stimulants, and the temporary idiocy of an inebriated man or woman has been transmitted and permanently embodied in the begetting and birth of a child that has been robbed of its rights by the wrongs of its parents, who have pulled down upon their own heads one of the most awful and prolonged curses which could be suffered as a result of a human mistake.

Note also carefully the fact that the exhausted physical condition of the bride is sure to result in an enfeebled offspring, should conception occur before she has regained her physical powers. It is possible that the exhausted physical condition of young brides, and that the excessive indulgence which is likely to follow the earlier months of marriage, either one or both, are largely the chief cause, or causes, of the frightful mortality among first-born children.

The joys of the newly-married are not only noticeable, but very beautiful. The outgoings of human affection are as beautiful and impressive as the relation of the birds that don their brightest plumage, sing their sweetest songs and build their nests in the springtime, when the mating instincts and emotional nature of the birds reach their highest and most animate expression. A young bride, in conversation with one of her intimate friends, in alluding to her happiness, said: "It is too good to last." The fact is, that this intensity of reproductive activity must give place to corresponding rest-periods of considerable length, or depletion and death would ensue as the inevitable result. The wave not only cannot, but it should not always remain at its crest, but it must subside and sink, in order that it may regain itself and rise on the crest of a new wave of emotional activity.

The pleasures of married life can only be heightened and perpetuated in a home of your own. The newly-married should always live apart by themselves, wherever such a course is at all possible. Living with the parents of either party is generally disadvantageous, and life in a hotel or boarding-house is not only undesirable, but dangerous.

Birds never live in a boarding-house, neither should married people. To the newly-married it is a place of special disadvantage and danger. They need to be alone, rather than under the constant gaze of the curious. In such a place both are exposed to the constant assaults of gossips, the wife is compelled to live in idleness, is a prisoner in her own room, is exposed to perils innumerable, and jealousies and alienations are likely to be engendered. A boarding-house is no place for the newly-married, who have a right to expect that lawful and honorable marriage may result in parentage. Any medical practitioner can testify to the number of young wives who have besought them to murder their unborn children because they were "boarding," and it was "not convenient to have a family."

A modest little home of your own is always best. If that is not possible, then rent a house, but do not start in a pretentious and extravagant way. Live within your means from the beginning. Do not bank upon the future. If you do not save money at first, the probabilities are that you never will. Debt is a terrible incubus. It will take the color out of the cheek of your wife, it will despoil the husband of pluck and energy and hope. It will cast over the prospect of coming years the dark shadow of despondency and despair. Cheerfully submit to such self-denials as will enable you to save something from your income. Join a good and safe building association, and if you cannot buy an humble home at once, plan to do so as early as possible. Plan for your needs and comforts, rather than for display and wretchedness. Home happiness is found in contraction, and not in expansion. A large house with many rooms requires the presence of many servants. These irritate, bring constant annoyance to the wife, who should be carefully delivered from undue anxiety; and they also impose large outlays of money, for which neither the husband nor the wife receive many returns, unless it may be the empty satisfaction of "what our friends will think." If you really wish your friends to think well of you, be governed by sense and not by sentiment.

For the sake of health, of present and future happiness, and the well-being of your children that are to be, both the husband and the wife should be industrious. His daily occupation and her daily duties will prove ministers of mercy to each. Idleness for either is a misfortune. Discontent, dissatisfaction and divorce, one or all, are always born of idleness.

Perhaps one of the happiest moments in your life will be when you step into a house which you can call your own home, and for the first time sit down at your own table. If you wish to perpetuate that joy, see to it that you are attentive, devoted, given to a verbal expression of your affection and an appreciation for every effort made by your wife to render your home attractive, your food palatable and your life enjoyable. Let her know that you appreciate every effort that she puts forth, and as the months and the years go by do not think a repetition of praise would become an offending monotony to her. A wife never ceases to love the expressions of admiration, appreciation and affection upon the part of her husband.

If you start out with a struggle to determine whether the will of the wife or the will of the husband shall have preference and pre-eminence, you may reasonably expect contention and strife for all the rest of your life. Let each seek to surpass the other in consideration, deference, and even self-denial, and the light and the joy which break upon your home in the beginning will abide to the end.

CHAPTER XI.

THE YOUNG WIFE AND MOTHERHOOD.

IN a previous place we have spoken of the importance of industry and activity as important elements in a young wife, and as essential in securing success for the family, happiness in the home, and bodily health and vigor for the wife. An idle woman is always an unhappy woman, and she eventually succeeds in making every one unhappy about her. Her household duties are no misfortune, but a blessing.

But there is also another side to the question. Unthoughtful husbands do not always appreciate the magnitude of the duties which fall to the successful homemaker and homekeeper. Her duties are legion. We do not now speak of the wives who live in affluence, who never need to regard expense, who have only to indicate their wish in order to have it executed; but of the great multitude of wives and mothers who preside in the homes of the great middle class and of those who struggle with the economies and duties in homes of small means. The young husband should appreciate the fact that if the beautiful poetry which adorns the tombstones in our cemeteries could be translated into truthful prose they would tell of the thousands of martyrs to mending, sewing, baking, scrubbing—they would tell that the weapons by which hundreds of these housekeepers were slain were the broom, the sewing-machine, the cradle and the ladle. The Thirty Years' War was not so severe or so prolonged as the warfare which is waged from early morning till late at night by the great army of industrious wives, busy mothers and anxious homekeepers. If the boy has lost his book or the girl her bonnet, mother must help to find it. If the baby coughs or cries at night the father sleeps on oblivious of the fact, but the infant cannot stir without being heard by its anxious and attentive mother. If sickness compels, she bends in anxious vigils over the little life that lies in the cradle. If the breadwinner is brought home sick, it matters not how manifold the duties of the mother, no trained nurse can take the place of the wife at the bedside. In health and in sickness, in prosperity and adversity, during the day and at night, the wife and the mother finds herself the centre of duties, and very often of exactions.

In the demands which a young husband makes upon the young wife he should remember what are her duties and requirements during the day, in the home, in the church, in society, in the community; he should remember that physically she is the weaker vessel, that even when in her best physical condition sexual inclination is largely dormant, and when she is weary and worn she deserves to be treated with more than usual thoughtfulness and consideration.

Whatever demands the young husband makes upon his wife, whether as his helper or the participant of his joys, he should remember that even from the low standpoint of selfish interest and personal pleasure he wrongs himself, in addition to being unjust and oftentimes cruel to his wife, when he fails to take into consideration her physical condition and manifold duties.

If the young husband and wife desire to be permanently happy they dare not ignore the special purpose for which God instituted marriage. While marriage has other purposes, yet the great final purpose is the raising up of a family and the perpetuation of the human race. The injunction which God gave to Noah, when he said, "Be ye fruitful and multiply, bringing forth abundantly in the earth, and multiply therein," is to-day, and ever will be, in force. Among the Israelites barrenness was regarded as one of the greatest of misfortunes. In many instances it was regarded as a cause of personal shame, and even of dishonor. When Hannah went up to the Temple and prayed for a son she was only giving expression to the longings and desires which filled the heart of every barren Israelitish woman who had entered into the sacred bonds of marriage, and when God promised Abraham and Sarah that their seed should be in multitude as the stars in the heavens they regarded themselves as the recipients of one of the greatest blessings which God could bestow.

The same is true in India, where the people are polygamists in theory, but seldom in practice, except when the first wife is childless. The family must not be left without a priest, or the parents without descendants; therefore the husband is permitted by law to take two, or even more, wives, in order that he may raise up children unto himself.

If marriage was instituted for the good of the man and the woman who enter into this sacred relation, their highest good cannot be attained in this relation until their union is blessed with children. It has been aptly said that the man needs the woman and the woman needs the man, and both need the children. The obligation to have children is not only enjoined in the Scriptures, but written in the physical, social and moral constitution of man and woman. This law is "rooted in the unconscious law of life which bids us perpetuate our kind; which guards over the conservation of life." "Love looks to marriage and marriage to offspring as a natural sequence." Any entering into the bond of marriage with the resolved purpose of avoiding the begetting and the bearing of children constitutes a union which accepts lust in the place of love, and converts the honorable estate of marriage into a form of legalized prostitution.

An earnest writer aptly says : " I must counsel husbands and wives to cherish the hope of becoming parents, and to let their hearts stand in a holy attitude in this respect. You should allow neither moderate income, financial pressure, sensual pleasure, nor evil forebodings, to cause you to entertain unholy thoughts or induce you to engage in criminal proceedings in this matter. No child should be considered an unwelcome intruder in the home. The heart of the home is the cradle; it is the cementing tie between husband and wife. God intends that husbands and wives should become parents; and no pure woman nor honorable man will enter upon matrimony with intentions to the contrary. If they do, God will visit upon them degraded morals, ruined health, financial loss, or other terrible inflictions. The world has millions of faithful wives and mothers, but there are thousands of childless wives who are so because they entered into that black crime of conspiring with the devil to prevent them from being mothers. They regard children as an unmitigated nuisance, and consequently darken, blast and damn their own lives with an act of murder. On the other hand, God blesses the mothers, in that he prolongs their days and brings up their children to reflect glory and honor upon them."

Dr. Guernsey says: "The object of marriage is the ultimation of that love which brings the two together and binds them together in the procreation and rearing of children for heaven. This is the only true aim and sole object about which every earthly desire, interest and plan of the married pair should cluster. No greater crime in the sight of heaven exists to-day than that of preventing the natural use of marriage. This is done in a great variety of ways, every one of which is criminal, in whatever form practiced; and none will escape the penalty—no, not one. Nature's laws are inexorable; every transgression, therefore, is surely punished, even at the *climacteric period*, if not before. The questions of failing health, or physical inability, or too frequent conceptions are matters for the investigation, advice and decision of an experienced, judicious and upright physician. They should never be taken in hand and judged upon by the parties themselves. And to the objection ' Can't afford to have children—they cost too much,' I have faith enough to reply, ' Our heavenly Father never sends more mouths than he can feed.' Let each one do his and her duty in life, and this cavil falls to the ground—which, when spilled, cannot be gathered up.

"Good people everywhere rejoice when they behold a married couple living together in an orderly manner and rearing a large family of children. How often is Queen Victoria held up as a pattern of excellence in this respect. She accepted and acknowledged Prince Albert as her husband and gave herself to him as his wife; and so indeed she was in every sense of the term. Although a queen, sitting on the pinnacle of power, she did not seek to avoid the pangs, the dangers or inconveniences of bearing children. By her own personal strength her twelve children were brought forth, and her own sensitive fibres and tissues felt the suffering. She nursed, caressed and loved them like a good mother, and she was a *royal mother!* Other kings and queens have done likewise; other husbands and wives, high in power, wealth and fashion, have done and are still doing the same. And how much the less should we, in the humbler walks of life, obey the divine command, 'Be fruitful and multiply'? If a husband truly loves his wife, and if she truly loves him, they will live for each other and in each other, and they will be one; and they will seek to do right in every particular of their marital relation."

We believe that every thoughtful man and considerate husband will concede that motherhood may not justly or properly be forced upon a resisting wife. That many wives do refuse to bear children, no well-informed person can deny. Sometimes the reasons assigned are unworthy of womanhood, base and ignoble. At other times the reasons assigned by the wife are worthy of the most thoughtful consideration. But whether the reasons which the wife entertains are honorable or dishonorable, correct or criminal, it must nevertheless be acknowledged that she is a free moral agent, and if she assumes the responsibility of declining one of the main purposes for which marriage was instituted she must herself bear the responsibility. To designedly inflict conception upon an unwilling and resisting wife the husband makes himself guilty of great injustice, invades the personal rights of his wife as an individual, and is guilty of a great wrong.

Where a wife is unwilling to become a mother, the best way for a husband to move her mind properly in this matter is to bring her under the influence of such books and teachings as will help her to understand her duty and obligation in this matter; help her to see that this is one of the great purposes for which marriage is instituted, and that where childbearing is intentionally and persistently evaded it becomes a crime against man and against God.

Many wives are not willing to consent to become mothers because they are unwilling to give up society; they prefer to live for the rounds of fashionable life. With others there is a dread of childbearing. This is not so common in brides or newly-married women; but with many, after they have given birth to one child they are unwilling ever to consent to a similar struggle. Had these young wives been made intelligent by their mothers, and been properly instructed upon these subjects before marriage, and lived according to the laws of hygiene and health during the period preceding the birth of their child, their experience might have been very different, and they would never have had the dread which comes to so many. There are good books upon this subject, and those who live hygienically and properly will find the terrors of childbearing greatly mitigated; indeed, they may be almost wholly alleviated. There are those who contend that childbearing may be rendered practically painless, and those who desire information upon this subject would do well to read the book entitled "Maternity Without Suffering," which is worth many times its cost.*

There are other women who dread the care and rearing of children, and there are still others whose aversion to childbearing is wholly due to their false ideas of life. To us, one of the saddest sights is a woman with a pronounced God-given mother-instinct who is unwilling to bear children, or, if she is the mother of children, is not willing to care for them, but thrusts them from her, committing them wholly to nurses and attendants, and then allows the mother-instinct to find its expression in petting a cat or mothering a dog.

No married woman should refuse to become a mother because of its perils. Statistics go to show that more unmarried women between the ages of twenty and forty-five die than of married women. God designed woman for motherhood, fitted her for its physical requirements, and her largest happiness, best health, greatest usefulness and longest life is attained by conformity to this divine purpose. Among the greatest sufferers in this world are the large numbers of those who have sought to defeat the purposes of God and have brought upon themselves untold misery. Obedience brings blessing. It is not only the end, but "the *way* of the transgressor" that is hard.

Parenthood is also essential to the rounding

---

* "Maternity Without Suffering," by Dr. Emma F. A Drake. Cloth binding. Price fifty cents. Published by the Vir Publishing Company.

out of the moral nature. That which is noblest and best in woman's nature is awakened and quickened when for the first time is folded to her breast a new life which is a part of herself. The child will teach her to be unselfish, to live for the happiness and well-being of another. Its government and discipline will awaken in her mind the principles which she desires to instil into the mind of her child, and as she gathers her little ones about her, tells them of God and heaven, and teaches them to lisp their infant prayer, her religious nature will attain unto a perfection and beauty which would not be possible under any other earthly influence.

The thoughtful and judicious wife also recognizes the fact that the presence of children in the home will exert an influence over the father which will refine, benefit and bless as no other influence on earth can. The little ones that reach out their hands in dependence toward him will inspire him to energy and effort in a higher, holier and nobler way than could ever be done by any commercial consideration. The noblest and most considerate manifestations of the father nature can in no other way be called into so full and beautiful an exercise as by the presence of children in the home. If the love for his children and the desire for their well-being and blessing do not teach him larger lessons of self-denial than he has ever known before, he will demonstrate that he is incapable of feeling the influence of the most potent incentive which God has permitted to come into human lives.

But the children will have an effect not only upon the parents individually, but they will bless both by drawing the husband and wife into a closer bond of sympathy and affection than would be possible under any other conditions. It has aptly been said that children are golden links that bind the husband and wife in a bond of closest endearment. They also serve as a buffer to break the jars of family life. These little ones awaken the best qualities in the natures of both parents. They enlarge and round out those qualities which would otherwise remain dwarfed and prematurely die. They afford a purpose in life for the father and mother, such as can be found in no other object upon earth.

In the study of their own children parents have an opportunity to learn human nature as they can learn it nowhere else. When their children are old enough they will criticise, suggest, and often help the parents to correct faults which would otherwise go unnoted and which could be properly criticised by no one else. It is the absence of this help which children bring into the home which oftentimes renders childless married people more faulty than others who have the advantage of such help. In times of trouble and trial the children will be prepared to comfort and sustain their parents. In times of sickness they will come with their sympathy and assistance, and when advancing years and the infirmities of age come they will be prepared to comfort and sustain their parents, and in their declining years afford them a refuge and a home, and when death comes they will shed the tear of sympathy and over their graves will plant the flowers that shall bloom in beauty and fragrance.

That the mother-instinct exists in the hearts of infants is early seen in the desire upon the part of little girls to mother their dolls, whether they have been purchased at great cost or are made of a few old clothes rolled up into the shape of a rag-baby. Where a stranger is uncertain about the sex of a child it can usually be pretty certainly determined by asking whether they prefer a doll or a horse.

It would be wrong, however, to suppose, because the little boy manifests the preference for a horse, that therefore he will never be interested in children. The pleasures and satisfactions of parenthood are as great to the father as to the mother, and while there is a difference between the mother-nature and the father-nature, yet, because of the terribly perverting influences of modern society, the desire for children is often stronger in the husband than in the wife. Where the natures of both are as God intended, sterility and barrenness would be alike a great disappointment for either. The desire for children is natural both to men and women, and in the home, as in universal nature, unfruitfulness and barrenness are a great misfortune.

About one marriage in eight or ten is usually barren of children. In the animal kingdom, and among insects especially, an abundance of food is indispensable to a rapid increase of numbers by reproduction. In the human family the question of food as it stands related to the question of reproduction is an important one. If the food is insufficient, either in quantity or quality, to maintain good physical conditions, or if it is too abundant or too rich, a tendency to sterility and barrenness is alike the result. Illustrations are not wanting of persons who, possessing large wealth and allowing themselves great indulgence in eating, became fat and corpulent and remained childless, but when financial reverses came their corpulence departed with their wealth, and they became the parents of children.

While the question of food is very important, it is not the only cause of barrenness. Sterility may be due to excessive sexuality in the marriage relation, or it may be due to such antenuptial indulgence of the husband as has resulted in a depleted condition of the reproductive organs. Sometimes it is due to apathy on the part of the wife, and at other times, although less frequent, it may be the result upon her part of too intense pleasure during coition.

It may also be due to abormal conditions produced by tampering with the reproductive function. In some instances there is a lack of such physiological compatibility as is necessary to result in conception. Instances are not wanting where barrenness has existed and the subsequent remarriage of both parties have demonstrated that neither were personally sterile, but that unitedly they were physiologically incompatible.

Barrenness is oftentimes the result of displacement of the womb or other unfavorable conditions in the female. It would be wrong, however, to suppose that the difficulty may not rest wholly with the husband. Even where a man seems in good bodily vigor and enjoys excellent health, the sperm may be devoid of those characteristics which are essential to the production of life. This condition can only be determined by a competent physician with the aid of the microscope and other means. It is also asserted by reliable medical authority that miscarriage may take place so early after conception that the wife may never suspect the real condition, but imagine herself sterile.

The cause of the barrenness of not a few women is clearly traceable to the fact that because of the impure life of the husband, either before or after marriage, he contracted gonorrhœa, and although at the time he may have thought it a small matter, and soon regarded himself as entirely cured, this terrible disease left its trace behind it, and perhaps two or three years afterward, when he entered the marriage relation, he imparted the hidden remnants of this disease to his innocent and unsuspecting wife, and in whom, perchance, the real disease has never been recognized at all, but the inflammation which it caused extended from the vagina to the womb, and then out through the tubes to the ovaries, and the delicate organs of reproduction were so injured as to result in permanent barrenness.

The cure for barrenness is found in remedying the cause. To discover what that cause is often requires the consultation and advice of a thoroughly competent physician, and to arrive at the most reliable conclusion a physical examination of the wife or the husband, or of both, may be necessary.

Where no means have been used to prevent conception, and the young wife has remained childless for a period of three years, there is adequate ground for a reasonable fear that causes exist, either in the husband or in the wife, which are likely to result in permanent sterility, and then no time should be lost to discover and remove the cause or causes.

The earlier years of married life are usually more fruitful than the years later on. Even where marriage is contracted after twenty-five years of age, the tendency towards sterility is easily perceptible. Marriage, either at too early or too late a period, tends to barrenness. Upon the part of the female the years from eighteen to twenty-four are likely to be the best years for marriage and maternity. Sometimes there is barrenness for a period of years, and this is followed by a period of quite frequent childbearing.

Barrenness may frequently be remedied by the exercise of great care upon the part of both the husband and the wife in the matter of diet and proper physical exercise. Sometimes a period of separation, varying from a few weeks to several months, is necessary to effect such physical changes as are requisite to the desired result. Single beds and separate apartments are sometimes essential, not only in order to secure conception, but to protect the beginnings of life from such disturbing influences as tend to produce the abnormal ejection of the embryo from its place of retention and growth in the womb.

CHAPTER XII.

QUESTIONS CONCERNING OFFSPRING.

It is natural that parents should long for children, and it is only proper that those who are barren should seek by all judicious and proper means to secure fruitfulness. But we are sorry to say that there is a widely prevalent and unnatural desire upon the part of many wives, and sometimes of their husbands also, to evade conception. This desire oftentimes leads these unnatural parents to seek the destruction of unborn human life. If the testimony of medical authority upon this subject is to be believed, this mania for child-murder is verily the "terror that walketh in darkness and the destruction that wasteth at noonday."

It is the duty of parents to protect the lives of their children, and the mother who desires or even consents to the murder of the infant in the cradle where God has placed it preparatory to its birth is as truly a murderer as when she strangles or stabs or poisons her infant in the cradle in which she has placed it after it is born. That the law recognizes the gravity of this crime is manifest by the fact that in nearly all the States of the Union this crime is regarded as murder, and punished accordingly. In some States, if the mother is proven guilty, the penalty is death, and in nearly all the States all who participate, have knowledge of, or assist, directly or indirectly, in producing such a result, are punished with imprisonment ranging from five to twenty years.

It has been supposed by some that where the beginnings of life are destroyed before the period of quickening, no crime is committed. This is a great mistake. From the moment that the spermatozoön penetrates the ovum and unites with it, life is present, and the destruction of that life is murder. The proposition is a very simple one. The only condition upon which the ovum may remain in the womb is by possessing life. As soon as it becomes dead it is rejected and cast out. If impregnated, while life continues in it, during its period of development, if nature is not interfered with, it is retained and nourished because it has life. The facts are simple enough: the germ is either dead or alive. If dead, nature casts it out; if alive, nature retains it. If nature retains it, and it is destroyed or removed by artificial means, the person or persons who produce such a result are guilty of murder.

There is no middle ground in this matter. Dr. H. S. Pomeroy, in his excellent book entitled "Ethics of Marriage," aptly says: "She who obtains a miscarriage at the earlier months of pregnancy feels comparatively virtuous because she draws the line at 'quickening.' This is moral jugglery and ethical hair-splitting; what evidence is there of soul at five months which may not be found at four? True, the unborn child of the latter age does not appear to move its legs and arms, while the other usually does. Is the spirit situated in the extremities, or is the movement of a muscle evidence of a soul? Considered from the low plane of physical life only, what reason is there for the distinction? There has been *life* from the first; there is no *independent life* until birth. It is reasonable to suppose that the Creator, who has been steadily at work for four months and fifteen days on one of the most delicate and complicated pieces in his whole laboratory, and has made no mistake thus far—the work being absolutely perfect as far as carried—considers it of little or no consequence to-day, but of the utmost importance and value when it shall have been in his hands a few hours longer!"

Dr. Napheys, in " Physical Life of Woman," says : " *From the moment of conception* a new life commences; a new individual exists; another child is added to the family. The mother who deliberately sets about to destroy this life, either by want of care, or by taking drugs, or using instruments, commits as great a crime, is just as guilty, as if she strangled her newborn infant, or as if she snatched from her own breast her six months darling and dashed out its brains against the wall. The blood is upon her head, and as surely as there is a God and a judgment that blood will be required of her. The crime she commits is *murder, child-murder*—the slaughter of a speechless, helpless being, whom it is her duty, beyond all things else, to cherish and preserve."

There is no division of opinion upon this subject. The world may hold up its hands in holy horror at the crime of Herod, but his crime is being perpetrated to-day in thousands of homes by "the slaughter of the innocents" at the hands of their own mothers. Dr. Pomeroy says: "We meet in our practice women who would hesitate to harm a fly, but who admit to having destroyed a half dozen or more of their unborn children, speaking of it as they would of the drowning of superfluous kittens." How are these thoughtless mother-murderesses to confront the souls of their unborn children on the day of Judgment? What of the declaration of Scripture, "Ye know that no murderer hath eternal life abiding in him"? While this passage of Scripture does not say that even a murderer may not be saved, yet it does say that one who commits murder is unsaved, and that salvation is not possible to him or her until they have sincerely repented.

The results of abortion are not only future and spiritual, but they are present, and affect serious temporal and physical results. Dr. Napheys says: "If they have no feeling for the fruit of their womb, if maternal sentiment is so calloused in their breasts, let them know that such produced abortions are the constant cause of violent and dangerous womb diseases, and frequently of early death; that they bring on mental weakness and often insanity; that they are the most certain means to destroy domestic happiness which can be adopted. Better, far better, bear a child every year for twenty years than to resort to such a wicked and injurious step; better to die, if need be, in the pangs of childbirth than to live with such a weight of sin on the conscience."

There can be no question but that many women are rendered incurable invalids by the violence which they do to nature by interrupting its work, destroying the growing life, and causing its expulsion in an unnatural way. Dr. Pomeroy aptly says: "Go into the orchard where there are ripe apples and others but half grown; try to pluck one of the latter; you pull, but it does not come; you twist this way and that way, and finally you secure a bruised apple with a torn and mutilated stem, and you leave behind a branch which bears unmistakable evidence of a violent and unnatural act. Turn now to the apples that are fully ripe; you put out your hand to take one, and as you touch it it falls gently and willingly into your open palm. If you now examine the stem and the branch from which it came you find no marks of violence; on the contrary, both will clearly show that nature had prepared for the separation.

"The two great dangers of childbearing are hemorrhage and fever; the first is caused directly and the second often indirectly by one and the same thing—the failure of the torn blood-vessel to close properly at the time of separation between mother and child. By the time the fruit is fully ripe Nature has so well arranged for this matter that the danger is small, but at an earlier period it is very considerable."

This attempt upon the part of parents to interfere with the order of nature has not only its terrible physical results for those who seek its perpetration, but it heaps upon the helpless unborn child terrible consequences from which it is powerless to escape. The attempt to destroy life is oftentimes a double failure. In spite of their murderous efforts, children are oftentimes born to such parents under circumstances which entail the most terrible and lifelong penalties. Children that might have been lovable in temper, companionable in disposition, healthy and happy, are born nervous, fretful and ill-tempered; and, because they were unwanted before they were born, the mother inflicts upon them a disposition which causes her ever after to wish they never had been born.

Something of what this result is will appear from a paragraph taken from an account by Helen H. Thomas, in "The Mothers' Journal," entitled "Unwanted," in which she thus narrates a visit to a friend:

"I found my friend half sick, and extremely nervous from lack of sleep, caused by her crying baby.

"But the child looked well, and the young mother assured me that it was constitutionally restless and out of sorts. She also said that she had lost more sleep since his advent—five months previous—than with all her other children—there are three of them—combined.

"After I had queried and wondered as to the why of it, for a time, the mother, with tears in her eyes, looked down at the little upturned face of the one cradled in her arms, and said:

"'It is all mother's fault, darling! She felt that her hands and heart were so full she had no room for you.' And then, looking me full in the face, she added, remorsefully: He is my only unwanted child! And so the dear little innocent suffers continually for my rebellious spirit prior to his birth. He seems restless and unhappy all the time; not at all like my other babies, who found a welcome awaiting them; and I realize now the mistake I made, in rebelling as I did, during those wearisome months, which I had planned so full of things which had to be put aside; and I am being punished for it, too. But I did not dream that by so doing I should bring suffering on my unborn child, as well as on myself."

Terrible as this picture may be, there is another thought which is still more terrible. When we remember that the mental condition of the mother during the period of gestation stamps itself upon the character of the child, what must be the character of a child who is born of a murderess—one who has either desired, planned for, or possibly undertaken and failed in the effort to murder her unborn child? How many of the murderers of to-day have inherited from their own mothers the predisposition to destroy human life? There is but little doubt that if the veil could be thrown off and the influence disclosed which molded the character and shaped the destiny of many of the children who are arraigned in the courts for the awful crime of murder, who seem possessed of an otherwise unaccountable predisposition to destroy human life, the terrible revelation would be made that during the period while their body was being formed and bent was being given to their character, prior to their birth, their mother was contemplating murder, and imparted this disposition to her own offspring.

Such thoughts not only mold the character of the unborn child, but they also affect the character of the parents themselves. The crime of child-murder must haunt them, and even if they do not suffer from the lashings of conscience, the moral character suffers irreparable damage.

But few persons are aware of the grave dangers which threaten health, and even life, when an abortion is performed. They are apt to think that it occasions only temporary inconvenience, from which they may recover in a few days, but all this is a very grave mistake.

Where accidental or unintentional miscarriage occurs, it is important both for the wife and for the husband to know that quite as much care needs to be exercised, and oftentimes for even as long a period, as for convalescence after confinement. A period of strict separation between husband and wife should be observed for a period of from six weeks to three months, according to circumstances. A failure to observe these necessities often results in serious and sometimes permanent disability upon the part of the wife.

The influences which prepare and pave the way in the minds of young women for the awful crime of child-murder are not difficult to find. One writer says: "The real beginning is in early life, when young people are taught, directly or by implication, that reproduction is a matter concerning which speech is indelicate, of which it is proper, even, to feel ashamed; as they grow older, and the period of marriage draws near, they learn to look upon parenthood as a responsibility and a burden which they may properly avoid if possible."

Parents are to blame for the total absence, during the education of their daughters, of proper instruction upon this subject. In the schools for the education of young women the course of study which has been especially arranged for the intellectual training and equipment of young men has been followed without being adapted to the special necessities of intelligent young women. They are taught many things which may serve a good purpose in securing mental discipline, but which are in every other respect impracticable, and, so far as the great purposes of their life are concerned, wholly useless. All the subjects which are best calculated to fit them for their intended position of wife and mother are studiously avoided;

they are kept in profound ignorance on all subjects of special physiology, and the question of maternity dare not so much as be mentioned by the professors in the class-room. What adds to this condition is the sad fact that parents do not supplement by personal instruction this lack of teaching in the school. Hundreds of young women are married who are so stupid as never to have asked where children come from, have no idea of the marital relation and the legitimate purpose for which God instituted the relation. When conception takes place, they do not know how to take care of themselves or prepare for the event which could be robbed of its terrors by intelligence. The birth of their first child is attended with such anguish and agony that forever after the marital relation becomes to them one of great dread, and to escape the condition which is so full of terror to them they resort to the destruction of unborn human life.

To correct this great wrong, the first and most essential step is the widespread dissemination of intelligence upon this subject. Marriage needs to be lifted into the light of a sacred and divine institution. The tenderest and most sacred relations of human life need to be preserved in their purity, so that pure-minded parents may speak of these relations without shame and blushing. Young women of mature years should be made familiar with the physiological conditions which attend conception and maternity, and they need to know that from the moment of conception life exists in the embryo, and that from the moment the spermatozoön enters and assimilates with the ovum a separate individual life is really begun, and that she is, at that very moment, the mother of this life within her as truly as when, in the later months, she feels the quickening within her, or after its birth experiences the joy of a mother who clasps her new-born infant in her arms.

But the crime of abortion does not rest wholly with the mothers. A large part of the guilt also belongs to the fathers. We may warn the wives against the terrible sin and awful physical consequences of abortion, but so long as husbands are unwilling to govern their passions, or to regulate their marital relations in harmony with the teachings of Scripture, but insist upon unlimited self-indulgence, the evils cannot be wholly corrected. Husbands need to be taught to look at the question from the wife's standpoint. The wrong is not all upon one side.

In a meeting of women only, after an address by a physician upon these subjects, a woman rose and said substantially as follows: " After I was married two years I became the mother of a puny, sickly baby. It required incessant care and watching to keep it alive. When it was only seven months old, to my surprise, astonishment and horror, I felt quickening, and for the first time I knew I was pregnant again. I was abased, humiliated! The sense of degradation that filled my soul cannot be described. What had been done? The babe that was born and the babe that was unborn were both to be robbed of their just inheritance. In tears and shame I told my mother, but she said: 'My child, why should you grieve and go on as you do? Don't you know that your children are legitimate?' My whole being rose in rebellion. I stamped my foot and almost screamed: 'Although my husband is the father of my children, they are not legitimate. No man-made laws, no priestly rites, can make an act legitimate that deprives innocent children of their right to life and health.' And then, with sobs and moans, reaction came, and I fainted in my mother's arms. What was the sequel? Two years later both of these children, after a brief existence, were lying side by side in the city of the dead, and until my husband and I learned the great laws which God has written deep in our being, we were not able to have children that could live."

The following somewhat lengthy but impressive quotation is from "Chastity," by Doctor Dio Lewis:

"Before we married I informed my husband of my dread of having children. I told him I was not prepared to meet the sufferings and responsibilities of maternity. He entered into an arrangement to prevent it for a specified time. This agreement was disregarded. After the legal form was over, and he felt he could now indulge his passion without loss of reputation and under legal and religious sanctions, he insisted on the surrender of my person to his will. He violated the promise at the beginning of our united life. That fatal bridal night! It has left a cloud on my soul and on my home that can never pass away on earth. I can never forget it. It sealed the doom of our union as it has done of thousands.

"He was in feeble health; so was I; and both of us mentally depressed. But the sickly germ was implanted, and conception took place. We were poor and destitute, having made no preparations for a home, ourselves and child. I was a stricken woman. In September following we came to ——, and settled in a new country. In the March following, my child, developed under a heart throbbing with dread and anguish at the thought of its existence, was born. After three months' struggle I became reconciled to my first unwelcome child. But the impress of my impatience and hostility to its existence previous to its birth was on my child, never to be effaced, and to this hour that child is the victim or an undesired maternity.

"In one year I found I was to be again a mother. I was in a state of frightful despair. My first-born was sickly and very troublesome (how could it be otherwise?) needing constant care and nursing. My husband chopped wood for our support. Of the injustice of bringing children into the world to struggle with poverty and misery I was then as sensible as now. I was in despair. I felt that death would be preferable to maternity under such circumstances. A desire and a determination to get rid of my child entered into my heart. I consulted a lady friend, and by her persuasion and assistance killed it. Within less than a year maternity was again imposed upon me, with no better prospect of doing justice to my child. It was a most painful conviction to me; I felt that I could not have another child at that time. All seemed dark as death. I had begged and prayed to be spared this trial again until I was prepared to accept it joyfully; but my husband insisted upon his gratification, without regard to my wishes and condition.

"I consulted a physician, and told him of my unhappy state of mind and my aversion to having another child for the present. He was ready with his logic, his medicines and instruments, and told me how to destroy it. After experimenting on myself three months, I was successful. I killed my child about five months after conception.

"A few months after this, maternity was again forced upon me, to my grief and anguish. I determined again on my child's destruction; but my courage failed as I came to the practical deed. My health and life were in jeopardy. For my living child's sake I wished to live. I made up my mind to do the best I could for my unborn babe, whose existence seemed so unnatural and repulsive. I knew its young life would be deeply and lastingly affected by my mental and physical condition. I became, in a measure, reconciled to my dark fate, and was as resigned and happy as I could be under the circumstances. I had just such a child as I had every reason to expect. I could do no justice to it. How could I?

"Soon after the birth of my child my husband insisted on his accustomed injustice. Without any wish of my own, maternity was again forced upon me. I dared not attempt to get rid of the child—abortion seemed so cruel, so inhuman, unnatural and repulsive. I resolved again, for my child's sake, to do the best I could for it. Though I could not joyfully welcome, I resolved quietly to endure its existence.

"After the birth of this child I felt that I could have no more to share our poverty and to suffer the wrongs and trials of an unwelcome existence. I felt that I would rather die at once, and thus end my life and my power to be a mother together. My husband cast the entire care of the family on me. I had scarcely one hour to devote to my children. My husband still insisted on his gratification. I was the veriest slave alive. Life had lost its charms. The grave seemed my only refuge and death my only friend.

"In this state, known as it was to my husband, he thrust maternity upon me twice. I employed a doctor to kill my child, and in the destruction of it, in what should have been the vigor of my life, ended my power to be a mother. I was shorn of the brightest jewel of my womanhood. I suffered as woman alone can suffer, not only in body, but in bitter remorse and anguish of soul.

"All this I passed through under the terrible, withering consciousness that it was all done and suffered solely that the passion of my husband might have a momentary indulgence. Yet such had been my false religious and social education that, in submitting my person to his passion, I did it in the honest conviction that in marriage my body became the property of my husband. He said so. All women to whom I applied for counsel said it was my duty to submit, that husbands expected it, had a right to it, and must have this indulgence whenever they were excited, or suffer, and that in this way alone could wives retain the love of their husbands. I had no alternative but silent, suffering submission to his passion, and then procure abortion or leave him, and thus resign my children to the tender mercies of one with whom it seemed I could not live myself. Abortion was most repulsive to every feeling of my nature, and at times rendered me an object of loathing to myself.

"When my first-born was three months old I had a desperate struggle for personal liberty. My husband insisted on his right to subject my person to his passion before my babe was two months old. I saw his conduct then in all its degrading and loathing injustice. I pleaded with tears and anguish, for my own and my child's sake, to be spared; and had it not been for my helpless child, I should have ended the struggle by bolting my legal bonds. For its sake I submitted to that outrage and my own conscious degradation. For its sake I concluded to take my chance in the world with other wives and mothers who, as they assured me, and as I then knew, were all around me, subjected to like outrages, and driven to the degrading practice of abortion. But even then I saw and argued the justice of my personal rights in regard to maternity and the relation that leads to it, as strongly as you do now. I saw it all as clearly as you do. I was then, amid all the degrading influences that crushed me, true and just to my womanly intuitions. I insisted on my right to say when and under what circumstances I would accept of him the office of maternity and become the mother of his child. I insisted that it was for me to say when and how often I should subject myself to the liability of becoming a mother. But he became angry with me, claimed ownership over me, insisted that I, as a wife, was to submit to my husband '*in all things*,' threatened to leave me and my children, and declared I was not fit to be a wife. Fearing some fatal consequences to my child or to myself—being alone, destitute and far from helpful friends, in the far West, and fearing that my little one would be left to want—I stifled all expression of my honest convictions, and ever after kept my aversion and painful struggles in my own bosom In every respect, as far as passional relations between myself and my husband are concerned, I have ever felt myself to be a miserable and abject woman. I now see and feel it most deeply and painfully. If I was with a child in my arms, I was in constant dread of all personal contact with my husband lest I should have a new maternity thrust upon me, and be obliged to wean one child before its time to give place to another. In my misery I have often cried out, 'O, God! is there no way out of this loathsome bondage?'

"It was not want of kindly feelings toward my husband that induced this state of mind, for I could and did endure every privation and want without an unkindly feeling or word, and even cheerfully for his sake. But every feeling of my soul did then, does now and ever must protest against the cruel and loathsome injustice of husbands toward their wives, manifested in imposing on them a maternity uncalled for by their own nature and most repulsive to it, and whose sufferings and responsibilities they are unprepared and unwilling to meet."

While we would not for a moment sanction the crime which this mother perpetrated, yet we are not prepared to say that she was the sole author of the crime. Every thoughtful man must admit that her husband was unreasonable, unwilling to govern his passion, cruel and unjust to his wife, and in his beastliness measurably drove her to the commission of the awful crime of which she was guilty.

The proper relation of husband and wife to the question of parenthood can never be properly and satisfactorily adjusted so long as either of these parties occupy extreme positions upon this question. It is absolutely wrong for the wife to take the position that she is to be wholly delivered from maternity and the care of children, and it is equally wrong for the husband to assume that the wife is created for no other purpose than to bear children in as rapid succession as nature renders conception possible. Upon the one hand it is the duty of the wife to arrange her thought and life with reference to maternity and the bearing of such a number of children as can be brought into the world in the highest state of physical, intellectual and moral equipment. Upon the other hand, the husband is to regard himself under obligation to practice such personal self-control and to bear such disadvantages as are incident to the greatest fidelity of the wife in her duties while the body and character of her child are being formed within her, and while it is being nursed, nurtured and cared for after its birth.

It is the grossest of insults not only to woman, but to her Maker, to assert that woman was created solely for reproduction. It is proper for a man in the discharge of certain duties and in the attainment of certain laudable ends to decline to marry and resolve to maintain a pure and celibate life throughout his entire existence; and it is equally right, and even commendable, for a woman with similar purposes and aims to decline marriage in order that she may devote herself with greater efficiency and success to some effort to elevate and bless mankind, if those ends could not be successfully accomplished in connection with the proper discharge of her duties as wife and mother. But when men and women do marry, they greatly mistake the object of this divine institution if they suppose that it was instituted solely for the purpose of producing the largest possible number of children—if they make *quantity* rather than *quality* the great purpose. Marriage was instituted for the highest good of the parents; it was instituted for the attainment of their best health and the largest intellectual and moral equipment. Their lives are to be shaped for the acquisition of the largest and best attainments. Unless they attain the best physical, intellectual and moral developments they cannot transmit these valuable qualities to their children. The children cannot inherit from the parents what the parents do not possess. Parents should seek to raise up, not the largest possible number, without regard to whether they are good, bad or indifferent; but there is no objection to their raising up the largest number consistent with the best possible equipment. One man is worth an innumerable number of monkeys, and we should seek to raise up not an innumerable horde of inferior beings, but only so large a number as is consistent with a sincere purpose not to evade the responsibilities and duties of parenthood, and with an earnest effort to raise up a race of superior men and women. There should be no consenting to deterioration, but a sincere desire and effort for the raising up of a new generation that shall be an advance upon all the generations that have preceded.

By what we have said it will be manifest that there is a culpable and criminal limitation of offspring; and there is also a reasonable and right regulation of the marital relation and a limiting of offspring—a designed and deliberate purpose to be self-contained with a view to intelligent, purposed parenthood.

There are times when it is positively wrong to beget and bring forth children. This is the case when there is such physical debility upon either the part of the husband or the wife as would render them incapable of transmitting or bearing healthy children; when, overburdened or broken down by excessive childbearing, nothing but puny, sickly, short-lived offspring could reasonably be expected; when the children are coming so rapidly that they interfere with each others' nutrition and imperil the mother's health, or when the mother is naturally so constituted that childbearing imperils her life. These, and other equally weighty reasons, are a sufficient justification for a careful study of duty and obligation in the matter of self-government, and the limitation, or even restriction, of childbearing by right and proper methods.

It is important, however, to say that married persons should never decide against childbearing, or even in favor of a very restricted parenthood, without the gravest considerations; nor is their own thought in the matter always sufficient to arrive at a wise and righteous conclusion. Their own judgment should always be supplemented by the counsel and advice of a well-qualified and thoroughly conscientious Christian physician. Where difficulties do exist, a conscientious consideration of them may often enable the parties to remove every barrier and secure the most blessed and gratifying results.

What we have intimated is aptly illustrated in the following instance given by Dr. Pomeroy in " The Ethics of Marriage ": " A 'love match' resulted in the union of two persons who were of nervous temperament and poor physique, many 'incompatibilities,' and small means. Beside this, the wife was suffering from a difficulty which made maternity undesirable and well-nigh impossible. Under the circumstances, they questioned whether indefinite postponement of parenthood were not proper, and, in fact, clearly indicated. They considered the matter carefully, took the benefit of medical advice, and finally decided that their only honorable and safe course would be that they should have a family of healthy children as its objective point. The wife was placed under medical treatment, and in the course of a few months was in physical condition safely to undertake maternity.

"Recognizing their limitations and disadvantages from the outset, the pair determined to make every possible effort to give their children as good a birth as might be, under the circumstances. Each tried to cultivate health and strength of mind and body; the laws of heredity were studied; conscientious care was taken that the mother might have bright and cheery objects about her and loving thoughts in her mind during the period when each child gained all its influence from the outside world through her. Each child was also, during this period, a subject of prayer, that the Holy Spirit might enter into its developing life and cause it to be so generated that the afterwork of regeneration might, if possible, follow as the day follows the dawn.

"It would be too much to say that this course would in every case be followed by results as marked as were those of this instance; but in this family the children have proved to be, if not all that could be desired, at least much better than would have been expected in the ordinary course of events.

"They were symmetrical, sound in body, equable in temperament, and affectionate towards the parents and each other. They have never been more than half the trouble and care that children ordinarily are, although possessed of high spirit and a keen sense of justice. What may develop as they arrive at maturity no one can tell, but it is certain that they now bear the impress of prenatal love and care, and a good birth. This cost the parents some effort and self-denial, but they have been repaid fourfold in the ease with which the nursery has been managed; moreover, little differences of taste and opinion were laid on the altar of sacrifice to the interests of the children who should be born to them, and each, as it joined in the family circle, brought new degrees of harmony and joy.

"I have repeatedly heard the father of that family declare that he had no reason to believe himself a dollar poorer than he would have been if no children had come to claim his care. Just what might have been in that case it is impossible to tell, but it is certain that many a childless marriage which began under apparently happier auspices than this one ended in misery and divorce."

But the question arises, where it is found necessary to limit the number of offspring, How shall it be properly done? There are those who seem to think that medical science has some way by which to grant unrestricted sexual indulgence and yet avoid the results which nature intended. Dr. Pomeroy says: "It is surprising to what an extent the laity believe that medical science knows how to control the birthrate. Just here let me say that I know of but one prescription which is both safe and sure, namely, *that the sexes shall remain apart*. So thoroughly do I believe this to be a secret which nature has kept to herself, that I should be inclined to question the ability or the honesty of any one professing to understand it so as to be able safely and surely to regulate the matter of reproduction for those living in wedlock."

Because of the moral issues, physical consequences and terrible results which cluster about this question—one of the most delicate with which we have to deal—we have made a most careful examination of this entire subject. We have read a great deal more than has been pleasant to our contemplation, but we have been compelled to return, after each new investigation, to the conclusion which is held by all reputable physicians that the only safe and sure way is for husband and wife to remain strictly apart. There are methods which are sometimes suggested, by even well-meaning physicians, to those who desire to escape the results of the marital relation, but when pressed for the expression of a candid and honest conviction these same physicians are always compelled to admit that for absolute safety there is but one provision.

These various methods are not only unsatisfactory and unavailing, but are ruinous in their effects upon the individuals who practice them. In some instances nature does not visit her penalties immediately, but eventually the old declaration proves true that although justice travels with a sore foot it is sure to overtake the transgressor.

Where married people are willing to live according to the laws which are written deep in our nature, they find what Dr. Kellogg has said is true: "There would be less sexual enjoyment, but more elevated joy. There would be less animal love, but more spiritual communion; less gross, more pure; less development of the animal and more fruitful soil for the cultivation of virtue, holiness and all the Christian graces."

An entire renunciation of all conjugal privileges is, however, only perfectly just and proper when it meets with the mutual consent of both husband and wife.

Concerning such a rigid course, Dr. Napheys, in "Transmission of Life," says: "The objection nowadays urged against it is that it is too severe a prescription, and consequently valueless. This ought not to be. A man who loves his wife should, in order to save that life overwork and misery, and danger of death and wretchedly constituted children, be able and willing to undergo as much self-denial as everyone of his contingent bachelor acquaintances does, not out of high devotion, but for motives of economy, or indifference, or love of liberty. The man who cannot do this, or does not care to do it, does not certainly deserve a very high position.

"But while all this is granted, the question is still constantly put: Is this all? Is there no means by which we can limit our families without either injuring the health or undergoing a self-martyrdom which not one man in a thousand will submit to?"

In meeting the perplexities of this situation, Dr. Pomeroy, in "Ethics of Marriage," says: "There are circumstances under which means for the *temporary* avoidance of conception may be desirable and proper, as, for instance, to prevent too rapid childbearing on the part of women who cannot nurse their infants, or who have their usual periods while nursing—conditions which, I believe, our artificial life are responsible for—and so are liable to too frequent conception.

"For such and other legitimate causes nature has herself provided a means which, with the practice of a little self-denial, will give a reasonable degree of safety; beyond this it is neither safe nor proper to act without the advice of some physician who has sound judgment, both in medicine and in morals."

There is a Scriptural provision which is doubtless designed to meet this very condition, and which may be properly mentioned here because authorized by the Inspired Word. The law concerning this matter will be found in the fifteenth chapter of Leviticus, beginning with the nineteenth verse. In this passage a period of strict separation is prescribed for the woman during the period of her monthly issue, and the injunction is, that when "she is cleansed from her issue then she shall number to herself seven days, and after that she shall be clean." On the eighth day she was to appear before the priest with her offerings, when she was to be declared clean.

In this Old Testament provision God manifestly intended to make the children of Israel intelligent, not for the purpose of enabling them to avoid any reasonable and right increase in their families, but measurably to limit the number of offspring, so that the very best type of human life might be the fruitage of their homes. When literally followed, it would doubtless in a large majority of cases afford all necessary relief, and properly limit the number of offspring.

This passage also clearly indicates the importance of separation during the periodic sickness; and the basis for this Old Testament teaching of separation during such times is based not only upon the sense of delicacy and propriety upon the part of the wife, but also upon the physiological and sanitary principles of medical science.

It is neither necessary nor proper for us to go into a further discussion of this subject at this place. Those who find themselves laboring under the burdens, infirmities and unfitness we have indicated, should be free to seek such medical counsel and advice as will afford them what relief may be available in their particular case. We would warn all, however, that "those who take active measures to prevent conception are apt to carry the matter further than they intended; at the best they are tampering with Nature, and that is a dangerous thing in itself." In seeking medical counsel, let us carefully advise all to exercise the utmost caution in selecting a competent, conscientious, Christian physician. If, however, you expect that your interview will bring you such information as will enable you to indulge your passion unrestrained and avoid all consequences, allow us to say, before such an interview takes place, that you are expecting information which medical science does not possess. Dr. Pomeroy, in writing upon this subject, says: "As before noticed, it is surprising to what extent the laity believe that the course of Nature can be safely interfered with, even by those who understand her laws the least. Those who fear to turn back the hands of a watch lest they injure the complicated and delicate machinery do not hesitate to use violent means to interfere with the natural workings of the human mechanism, which is a thousandfold more complicated and delicate. Nature is tenacious of her rights; she resists grandly, but if forced to yield, she visits the offender with punishment which is no less sure because it is sometimes long-delayed. Few seem to know this; many act as though they considered Nature a sort of clever idiot, too stupid to recognize an injury or too amiable to resent it if discovered; while others seem to look upon Nature as rather intelligent and able, but a servant amenable to guidance and assistance in co-ordinating the forces of her laboratory. This is absurd, and even impious, for Nature is but another term for the Creator of all things, and He is infinitely wise. Nature cares more about correcting *us* than our mistakes and follies. Were she to go on indefinitely and patiently undoing our work we should go on indefinitely and persistently doing it, and our wrongdoing would be righted, but we should remain in the mental or moral or physical sin which had prompted it. Indeed, if the obvious results of our sin were promptly removed we should scarcely be aware that we were not in harmony with Nature's plans, and the race would deteriorate, and finally become extinct."

Where you do not obtain from a reputable, intelligent Christian physician the information you desire, or the relief you seek, do not make the fatal mistake of resorting to some quack or impostor who advertises only to beguile, deceive and rob you, and subsequently to leave you humiliated, with purse depleted and health ruined. Reputable physicians do not advertise, and the very fact that a man advertises may be accepted as sufficient evidence that he is not an accredited and reliable physician, and that you will most assuredly be subjected to deception and imposture.

Persons who recognize the propriety of limiting the number of offspring are seriously exposed to the danger of deferring and procrastinating to such an extent as to err greatly in the direction of too few rather than too many children. With most women the time for childbearing is quite like the time and location of a boil—any other time than the present, and any other place than where it is. A purposed parenthood is in *danger* of becoming a purpose to evade parenthood.

There is, however, a proper and all-important preparation for parenthood. After a careful examination of the subject no person can help but be deeply impressed with the fact that if the parents of this generation would realize their wonderful power to mold and fashion the succeeding generation, the children of the next decade would rise to the level of an entirely new plane. Some people seem to think that the matter of begetting a child, like the matter of selecting a wife or a husband, should be left wholly to blind chance. Neither of these two important events can be too much safeguarded by wise and thoughtful consideration. If conception is permitted to take place when either one or both of the parents are in ill health; if the wife is an unwilling mother, and the embryo is developed by her while her entire nature rebels against the admission into the family of a child who is not wanted, the children begotten and born under such circumstances can never be other than sickly, nervous and fretful during their entire childhood, and cross and uncompanionable throughout their entire lives.

In connection with childbearing there are three very important things: First, the preparation for parenthood; second, the mental state at the period of conjunction, and third, the mental state and physical condition of the mother during the months while the body and character of the child are being fashioned within her body.

The period and the character of the preparation for parenthood must always vary according to the physical condition of the intending parents. In some instances this preparation needs to extend over weeks, and in other instances even over years. No man or woman should consent to become a parent except at such times when physically and intellectually they are at their very best—indeed, the very best that is possible for them to attain by a course of careful preparation. Much of what might be said here will be learned under a subsequent chapter upon pre-natal influences.

Medical authorities universally attach great importance to the mental condition at the moment of conjunction and conception. It is quite universally believed that this is a moment of unparalleled importance to the welfare of the future being. Dr. Hufeland, an eminent German writer, says: "In my opinion, it is of the utmost importance that this moment should be confined to a period when the sensation of collected powers, ardent passion, and a mind cheerful and free from care, invite to it on both sides." It is an awful crime to beget life carelessly, and when in improper and unworthy physical and mental states.

The ancients understood the importance of this moment, and frequently surrounded the nuptial couch with statues which should charm the mother by their beautiful outlines and physical proportions. It was claimed by them that a man who was himself deformed might in this manner become the father of children that were possessed of fine physical proportions. While this statement might carry with it too much presumption, yet it was not without a considerable element of truth.

Nearly eighteen centuries before Christ, the patriarch Jacob recognized this principle when he arranged with Laban to accept from among the flocks and herds "the speckled and the spotted" as the reward of his labor in attending the flocks of the herds of his father-in-law. There was nothing unnatural or miraculous in the result which Jacob secured. He sought to produce such mental impressions upon the minds of the flock at the time of conception as would secure the production of young marked after the manner most in accord with his personal interests. We are told that "Jacob took him rods of green poplar, and of the hazel and chestnut-tree, and pilled white streaks in them and made the white appear which was in the rods. And he set the rods which he had pilled before the flocks in the gutters in the watering-troughs, when the flocks came to drink, that they should conceive when they came to drink. And the flocks conceived before the rods, and brought forth cattle ring-streaked, speckled and spotted. And Jacob did separate the lambs, and set the faces of the flocks toward the ring-streaked, and all the brown in the flock of Laban: and he put his own flocks by themselves, and put them not unto Laban's cattle. And it came to pass, whensoever the stronger cattle did conceive, that Jacob laid the rods before the eyes of the cattle in the gutters, that they might conceive among the rods. But when the cattle were feeble he put them not in: so the feebler were Laban's, and the stronger Jacob's. And the man increased exceedingly, and had much cattle, and maid-servants and men-servants, and camels and asses."

Much of the differences which exist between children of the same parents may be easily attributed to the different bodily and mental conditions of the parents at the period of conjunction, the changed physical, intellectual and emotional states of the parents at the different periods of conception producing the corresponding differences in their offspring.

The results of purposed and prepared parenthood are so great and so desirable that a husband and wife should consider these matters carefully, make due preparations, and approach the period when they would beget offspring and bring immortal beings into the world with the greatest thoughtfulness, consideration, and also with prayer.

The writer well remembers the deep impression made upon his mind in an interview with a physician who was the first to present this phase of the subject to our consideration. The statement was so unusual that it made a lasting impression upon us. But why may it not be so? After a period of preparation why should not the intending parents unite at the throne of grace for God's blessing upon them in the act in which they are about to engage, and in the fulfillment of their desire for an heir who shall be possessed of the very best physical, intellectual and moral endowments?

There are certain signs of fruitful conjunction which are often recognized by women who are already mothers, but which may serve as no guide to a young wife who has never had any experience. With some women the act of conception is attended with great emotion, a sense of unusual pleasure, and even of a tremor, in which all parts of the body may participate. Sometimes it is followed by a sense of weakness. In ancient times the swelling of the neck was regarded as a sign of conception, and some modern authorities incline to the same theory. There are instances also in which the morning sickness begins immediately after conception.

It would be unsafe, however, to rely upon either the presence or absence of these indications. In most instances the cessation of the menses and the appearance of the morning sickness are the first reliable indications that conception has taken place.

CHAPTER XIII.

THE EXPECTANT MOTHER.

A HUSBAND, whether young or old, should treat his wife with great consideration at all times, but if at any time she deserves more thoughtful consideration and more tender ministry than at any other, it is during the period of her pregnancy. The young husband should remember that oftentimes the mother-nature of the young wife is not yet aroused, but is measurably dormant. God has intended that wifehood should precede motherhood. Where the longing for children is present, the young wife intelligent, and where she has been physically fitted for the office of motherhood upon which she has now entered, her equipment is exceptional, her mind complacent, and she may reasonably be expected to go forward in a spirit which will secure for her in the coming months the largest blessing and reward.

But with most young wives it is not so. The knowledge which would have been most important for them has been withheld by silent mothers. They may have received a liberal education, but in the study of physiology, the special parts, concerning which she needed most to know, have been excluded from the text-books, and she knows no more concerning her own special physiology than she does about the physiology of the male. Books which would have rendered her intelligent have been studiously kept out of her sight, and perhaps during her girlhood she has been encouraged in compressing her waist, displacing the vital organs which God has placed in the abdomen, and through a period of years gone on, ignorantly or wilfully, unfitting herself for the main duties of maternity. Perhaps she has entered upon marriage, as so many do, with an undefined dread of some impending evil attending conception and childbearing, which she has desired and hoped to escape in some inscrutable manner. The discovery of the fact that she is to become a mother fills her mind with dread and alarm. In her ignorance she gropes her way in darkness, not knowing whither to turn and with no one to guide her to the light. She naturally turns to married women and to mothers, and instead of receiving encouragement and the proper kind of sympathy, they most likely exclaim: "I am sorry for you! Now your trouble begins. If I were in your place I should feel like jumping into the river." In nine cases out of ten, with the darkness intensified and her mind more alarmed than ever, apprehension turns to fear, and fear into alarm and dread. The young husband should remember that this is about the usual experience of most young wives, and intelligently arrange to correct the evil.

If you are acquainted with some intelligent,

sympathetic and judicious woman, who will know how to take your young wife into her arms, allay her fears, comfort and instruct her, you will be most fortunate. She should be able to point out to the troubled wife the fact that intelligence and care will greatly mitigate, and indeed enable her largely to avoid all physical suffering; to explain to her how, as the months go by, the mother-love will spring up in her heart as the time approaches for the happiest hour in her life, when for the first time her own infant child shall lie in her arms or by her side; to picture the joy of her husband and the gladness which will come into the hearts of all who know her and who will come to rejoice over her newborn child; to picture what her home will be as contrasted with those who, dejected and lonely, sit in desolate homes where no little prattler breaks the stillness of the hours and no footfalls are heard in the hallway. This judicious friend will need to know how to impress upon her that her mental condition during the period which precedes the advent of the little stranger will mold and fashion its character, and how, if she desires a loving child, she must herself love the child before it is born; if she desires in her child a quiet and happy disposition she must herself determine that result by her own even temper, and be warned that her worry and repining will render her child nervous and fretful; if she desires her child to be cheery and bright and happy she should enact in her own thought and life what she desires her child to be; that now for a brief period she is molding not simply its physical frame, but its character and disposition, and giving bent and expression to the entire future of the human life that is being formed within her.

It will not do, when the husband finds his wife despondent, that he should be annoyed by expressions which are quite natural to one in her condition. No young husband can enter sufficiently into the sufferings and feelings of his wife in these earliest days and weeks of apprehension and dread. She needs to be comforted with words of greatest tenderness. Your heart should go out toward her in sincere sympathy. Put away from your heart such feelings as, "Foolish girl! What did she get married for? Did she not know that she was expected to bear children, like other women? She is not suffering more than other women have suffered. All this is only in the course of nature. What use is there of making a fuss? She should submit to it in the proper spirit." If you harbor such thoughts, whether properly or improperly, they will nevertheless unfit you for that degree of sympathy which you should feel and not feign.

The months of pregnancy with most women are months of discomfort. Some women are in better health, more cheery and hopeful during the period of gestation than at any other period in their lives. But this is not generally the case; rather the reverse. During gestation some women are a terror to their husbands, and render themselves miserable, and all about them uncomfortable and unhappy. During this period the wife ceases to be physically attractive, and for her own protection and the protection of the embryo, nature makes the wife sexually repellant. Soon the morning sickness is likely to begin, and when she rises in the morning she will likely feel sick and nauseated, and vomiting will frequently ensue. Relief cannot always be afforded, and this condition may continue for weeks, or even for months. The young wife soon becomes the target for all kinds of injudicious advice. She is told to eat heartily of strong food, to "keep up her strength," and " to furnish nourishment for two." Her natural modes of life are oftentimes unnecessarily restricted, and after a period, with a sense of false modesty, she often shuts herself out from fresh air and exercise, and becomes a prisoner in her own home, or possibly in her own room.

While the pains and perils of maternity can be greatly mitigated, yet the young husband should be moved to tenderest consideration because of the discomforts which the wife suffers ; the apprehensions with which she looks forward to the hour of her delivery, the responsibilities of caring for and rearing a child for usefulness in this world and happiness in the next ; the apprehensions which she may have, not only in regard to her own life, but in bringing into the world a creature who shall be dependent for many years upon her and her husband ; and in the days of her nervous anxiety she is likely to think of the possibility of the death of her husband, or, of what might be even more terrible to her thought, her sickness or disability through a period of years, when the breadwinner himself might become dependent upon his wife and children for his own support.

Newly-married persons should look forward to this period, and, before conception takes place, make themselves the possessors of such information as would render them intelligent and qualify them to meet the conditions with the best physical and intellectual equipment. When the wife has once become pregnant, it is then too late for her properly to take up the study of this subject. Instead of permitting her mind to dwell upon these matters, her attention should be turned to other considerations. If she or her husband have not read upon these subjects until the event takes place, then the husband should devote himself to the reading, and be to his wife a wise counsellor in the experiences through which she is passing. He should carefully study the book entitled "What a Young Wife Ought to Know," and possibly other well-chosen books. Where the husband has the time and the technical knowledge, he might find it very helpful to consult the physician whose services they expect to have at the time of confinement, and borrow from him a medical work upon the subject. Such books are always expensive, and, although written in technical terms, may yet prove interesting and suggestive. The greatest danger, however, in this course is, that medical books deal not so much with the *normal* conditions which characterize the vast majority of confinements, but with the abnormal and exceptional, which are only occasionally met, and these exceptions, abnormal conditions and hideous monstrosities, are likely to fill the mind with unnecessary apprehension. Under no circumstances should a pregnant wife be permitted to fill her mind with apprehension and alarm by reading of this character.

If the wife is to follow the most beneficial rules of exercise, diet and mental condition, she will need to be encouraged and assisted by the judicious counsel and tenderest sympathies of her husband. If she is allowed to seclude herself and become inactive, she will not only suffer the severest experiences at the time of delivery, but her child will be likely to be indifferent to physical and intellectual activity; while, upon the other hand, if her life is filled with a round of perpetual duties, perplexities and worries which consume her time, leave her depleted, and allow her no time for rest, she is likely to be the mother of a restless, nervous and irritable child. The young husband should remember that what his home is to be in the days to come will depend upon the intelligence and wisdom of himself and wife while they stand at the sources of destiny in the early period of their married life. Their health, their wisdom, their judicious direction is to determine not only their own present happiness but the character of their children, the condition of their home, and measurably even the destinies of generations yet unborn.

It is not within our province, when writing to young husbands, to lay down rules and to give full directions which are fitted for a book of instruction to young wives and expectant mothers. But as something might be properly expected upon this phase of the subject, we append from "Trained Motherhood" a suggestive article on "Diet and Hygiene for Expectant Mothers," by a writer who signs herself "K. L.":

"From the very moment of consciousness of the conception of a new life every effort should be made for the welfare of both mother and child.

"With the majority of women pregnancy is a condition to be dreaded, since it brings with it so much care, pain and all sorts of trials, ending with intense suffering.

"The greater part of these troubles are caused by the violation of the laws of nature; and by following a few simple rules much, if not all, of the suffering and worry women undergo may be avoided.

"Having received many requests for advice, the writer gives, for the benefit of sister women, as the result of personal experience and experiments, the directions and hints that follow:

"One of the chief causes of trouble is improper diet. Another is improper dress. A third, lack of exercise.

"But to deal with one at a time, we will place

diet first. It is necessary that a pregnant woman should have food that is nourishing but not heating for the blood. It should be eaten at regular hours and in moderate quantities. Very few people can successfully eat and drink at one time, so it will be much better to drink some time before or after meals. It is desired to avoid development of bone and muscle, as it is this growth that renders the labor so hard. By choosing food that lacks these qualities much trouble may be avoided. All the vegetables and all the fruits are beneficial, but all animal food is injurious, in my opinion.

"All rich food, such as pastry, cakes, confectioneries, gravies and fat meats should be avoided. Tea and coffee are nerve and brain stimulants, therefore injurious to both mother and child. Wines or liquors of any sort are very much to be condemned. All cereals may be used freely, though the oat products are not to be so well recommended as the wheaten grains, since oats are more heating. Eat very freely of all fruits, particularly the acid sort. Oranges and lemons stand first, then apples, peaches and plums. Bananas are very good, especially when eaten in the morning before taking other food. Be sure and not eat too much of anything. It is better to feel a little hungry than to eat an ounce too much. Those who desire a warm drink may find some cereal coffee palatable and beneficial. Whole wheat or brown breads are more desirable than white breads, as they contain less starch properties.

"The 'morning sickness' may be done away with by eating several plain crackers—soda or graham—before rising. Eat them while lying down, and lie still for five minutes. Then get up slowly and gently. The juice of a lemon or a banana will often do the same towards removing this weakening annoyance. Generally if fruit is eaten just before going to bed, no nausea is felt in the morning.

"As to dress: No garment should be worn that throws any weight or pressure anywhere. Hang all from the shoulders. A corded waist with shoulder-straps, and buttons for the skirts, will be comfortable. By all means have everything as light in weight as possible. Dress warmly, but let nothing be tight or heavy. Wear low-heeled, broad-soled shoes, so as to keep the legs and feet from swelling under the strain of the extra weight they must carry.

"Plenty of judicious exercise is necessary. Housework and light gardening are unequaled, though the heavier work, such as washing, scrubbing or lifting, reaching up, pulling, or any kind of strain, is dangerous. Climbing stairs and hills is one of the best exercises. Breathe deeply and fully, filling the lungs all the way down. The majority of women only breathe with the upper part of their lungs, and have no chest expansion. A healthy woman ought to be able to increase her chest measure at least two inches by a full inhalation. Deep breathing not only gives the mother more strength, but it gives the unborn child a gentle exercise by means of the motion of the mother's body at each breath, and renders its whole system purer and stronger. Keep the mouth closed, and this forces deep breathing. Climb hills and stairs with mouth shut, head well up, shoulders back, and breathe as fully as possible while climbing.

"Exercise freely, but do not overdo it. Any fatigue drains from the fetus its vitality and development, which is its birthright, and which is the duty of every woman to give her child.

"A tepid sitz bath, taken for fifteen minutes just before going to bed, will induce sound, refreshing sleep, and at the same time keep the parts pliable and soften the muscles. Dry thoroughly and cover warmly, to avoid risk of chill. Frequent bathing in cold water will keep the circulation good, and should always be followed by gentle rubbing with a rough towel. Massage with olive oil will remove any tendency to a tension of the skin as it is distended.

"A strong solution of alum applied to the nipples each night, and allowed to dry on, will harden the skin and prevent soreness from nursing.

"Maintain as erect a position at all work as possible, as stooping brings pressure where it will do the most harm.

"It is best to wait until the third day at least after the child is born before changing the diet, and then the mother should eat freely of all that she has avoided during pregnancy, in order to give her milk the qualities the child now needs.

"As it is the duty of all parents to give to their children the very best of themselves, the only way to do this is to give them the care before their birth that they intend giving them after birth.

"In evidence of the benefits of this diet, compare these two experiences of the same mother:

"*Mixed diet*, rich foods of all kinds, poor hygiene, incorrect exercise. Result, ten-pound child; fifteen hours labor, very severe; mother sat up for the first time on tenth day.

"*Fruit diet*, all the preceding rules followed. Result, seven and one-half-pound child; labor one hour, not at all severe; mother sat up eight hours after; up and dressed on the sixth day. Perfect health after, for both mother and child."

We can heartily endorse the directions of the writer in every particular, but think it important to suggest that some of the greatest mistakes made after confinement are by impatience to have the mother enjoy the privilege of sitting up, going to the table for her meals, and returning to the ordinary duties of daily life. We have elsewhere indicated the changes which take place at this period, and which call for an entire revolution in the physical condition of the mother. This cannot be accomplished in a few days, or even in a couple of weeks. In most instances it is safe for the young mother to expect to remain at least six weeks in her room before thinking of being a guest at the family table. A mistake at this time may eventuate in permanent results which will render the mother an invalid for all the rest of her life.

But there is another side to this question which cannot be passed over at this point without great injustice to the sacredness and importance of the subject. The self-denials and trials during the period of gestation do not all fall to the lot of the wife. With her the sexual sense has been satisfied and has become quiescent, while in the husband it continues active, and sometimes even seems imperious. If he is to treat his wife with proper consideration he should allow nothing to stimulate or excite his sexual passion, but should be able to hold himself in the best physical poise and under the wisest sexual self-control.

Any one who has observed the life of birds and animals, and indeed of all animate life, cannot have been blind to the fact that after impregnation the female never receives the male, and the male, neither of beast or bird or reptile, never forces himself upon the female; while the young life is being developed in the body of the female the sexes remain absolutely apart. If we are to learn anything from universal nature in this particular, we would seem to be taught that the same should be true with husband and wife.

It is a notable fact that among the heathen in polygamous countries the husband always remains apart from a wife in whom life has already been begun. Strange to say, in civilized and Christian countries medical writers and intelligent people are not always in accord. That the reader may understand something of the positions which are taken, we quote from a few well-known writers:

In his book entitled "The Physical Life of Woman," Dr. George H. Napheys says: "During those days when the wife, if she were not pregnant, would have been 'unwell,' marital intercourse should be abstained from. It is then injurious to the mother and dangerous to the life of the child, as it is liable to excite miscarriage. But if this habitual epoch of the monthly sickness be avoided, there is no reason why passion should not be gratified in moderation and with caution during the whole period of pregnancy. There is one exception to be made to this general course of conduct. In those cases in which a miscarriage has occurred in the first pregnancy, every precaution should be employed to prevent its happening again after a second conception. Under such exceptional circumstances, therefore, the husband and wife should sleep apart during the first five months of pregnancy. After that period their ordinary relations may be resumed. When a miscarriage has taken place, intercourse should not be permitted within a month of the accident. The observance of this direction is of the utmost importance. Its neglect is the frequent cause of severe and intractable diseases of the womb."

Another, when speaking of the effects of coition during this period, says: "The organ of amativeness is frequently too largely developed in the embryonic offspring by the excessive indulgence of parents in sexual pleasures during the period of gestation. After the birth of the child, he is usually fed on meat, tea and coffee, and other stimulating food and drink, fit only for persons of adult age, by which sexual precocity is produced."

Dr. John Cowan, in "The Science of a New Life," says, with emphasis: "I will again repeat that during this full period of gestative influence, as well as during the period of nursing, *sexual congress should not be had between husband and wife.* This is the law of Nature, the law of God, and outside of Christendom it is never violated. Animals will not permit it—savages will not permit it, and over three-quarters of the world it is looked upon as infamous by our own species. A man acting out the licentiousness of his nature with his wife during gestation is worse than a brute—in fact, there is no species of the animal to which he can be compared, unless it be to the tobacco, whiskey-soaked hanger-on to a rum-shop—whose life is an epitome of tobacco, whiskey and licentiousness. Do not, I pray you, oh, parents, do this unclean thing. Do not taint your clean bodies, do not foul your pure souls with the lustful of your natures, while a new body is being developed, a new soul being organized; but by sweet words, loving caresses, endearing action and warm kisses cultivate within you the love element that, in its pure exercise, joins together two souls, and brings in its path such a measure of peace and happiness as must be realized ere it can be appreciated."

Writing of the physical needs of the mother during the period of gestation, Dr. Napheys says: "During this period the whole force of the economy at these times is taken up with providing sustenance for the new being, and there is no nervous power left to be wasted in barren pleasures. In those exceptionable cases where this does not hold, every excitement is visited upon the child, and it has to suffer in health and growth for the unnatural appetite of the mother."

Dr. J. R. Black says: "Coition during pregnancy is one of the ways in which the predisposition is made for that terrible disease in children, epilepsy. The natural excitement of the nervous system in the mother by such a cause cannot operate otherwise than inflicting injury upon the tender germ in the womb."

Dr. J. H. Kellogg says: "Indulgence during pregnancy is followed by the worst results of any form of marital excess. The mother suffers doubly, because laden with the burden of supporting two lives instead of one. But the results upon the child are especially disastrous. During the time when it is receiving its stock of vitality, while its plastic form is being molded, and its various organs are acquiring that integrity of structure which makes up what is called constitutional vigor—during this most critical of all periods in the life of the new being, its forces are exhausted and its structure is depraved, and thus constitutional tendencies to disease are produced by the unnatural demands made upon the mother."

The same author adds: "Still another terrible consequence results from this practice so contrary to nature. The delicate brain, which is being molded with the other organs of the body, receives its cast largely from those mental and nervous sensations and actions of the mother which are the most intense. One of the most certain effects of sexual indulgence at this time is to develop abnormally the sexual instinct in the child. Here is the key to the origin of much of the sexual precocity and depravity which curse humanity. Sexuality is born in the soul of a large share of the rising generation."

In her book, entitled "Tokology," Dr. Alice B. Stockham says: "If the law of continence is not the law to govern one's entire life, it is natural and reasonable that the mother should be exempt from the sexual relation during gestation."

In an excellent little book, entitled "Approaching Maternity," a physician of experience says: "A man once told me that the easiest delivery his wife had ever had took place two days sooner than expected, and one day after he had had connection with her! Thank heaven, there are not many such brutes as this! What really took place was a miscarriage, in my opinion, superinduced by coition. That it was not troublesome was a piece of good luck, and must have been the result of the woman's excellent condition. It is better that during the entire pregnancy sexual intercourse should be abstained from. During coition the uterus is subjected to great disturbance; congestion of many of the parts follows, and the effect upon the nerves is of a harmful nature. The entire vital energy of the woman is needed and should be saved for the coming event, and the husband should practice self-control and forego selfish indulgence at this time. Strive rather to elevate and develop the intellectual side of the woman, and if her mind is kept occupied upon helpful, entertaining subjects, a good result will show later on."

When we remember that in procreation God has endowed us with the power to continue his work of creation and realize the sacred responsibilities in calling a new life into being, we cannot but feel that from the very hour of conception the mother is overshadowed by the Most High. In the fulfillment of her sacred office she should surely be delivered from all polluting intrusions, and be permitted to live a life of spotless purity. To say the very least, there surely is something very suggestive in the statement of the first chapter of Matthew concerning the parents of the child Jesus. When he had been begotten of the Holy Ghost, Mary was not to be deprived of the companionship, love and sympathy of Joseph, and therefore when he thought to put her away privily, he was told "fear not to take unto thee Mary thy wife, for that which is conceived in her is of the Holy Ghost."

" Then Joseph being raised from sleep did as the angel of the Lord had bidden him, and took unto him his wife, *and knew her not till she had brought forth her first-born son.*" While it was essential that the fatherhood of the Messiah should be above all question, yet may it not be true that the development and bringing forth of a child which shall be most like unto this Prince of Peace always demands an undisturbed maternity?

We would not like to take an extreme position upon this subject, but we are persuaded that what we have presented here is worthy of the thoughtful consideration of all husbands and wives who seek their own highest good and the greatest blessing and well-being of the children which are to be.

It is well for young husbands and wives to know that by incautiousness in their relations during this period miscarriage is often easily and actually produced, and unsuspecting parents have oftentimes been the authors, not only of the death of their own child, but the consequences have entailed permanent injuries upon the young wife, and oftentimes resulted in death itself.

CHAPTER XIV.

THE CHANGES WHICH PRECEDE, ATTEND AND FOLLOW CONCEPTION AND CHILDBIRTH.

From the moment of conception, during the months of gestation, at the time of childbirth and after, changes of great interest take place in the germ of human life and in the body of the mother. Her body is marvelously fitted for the reception and development of the ovum, the embryo and the fetus through the various stages of fertilization, germination, development, maturity, to the time of the eventual exit of the child into the outer world to begin its own independent life.

Something of the adaptation of the body of the mother to its marvelous purpose may the better appear if we think of some of the greatest mechanical achievements of man.

A watch is one of the best products of human ingenuity. It has taken nearly six thousand years to produce it. It is a wonderful piece of mechanism, yet it is, after all, not a complex product like the human body. If a watch could be constructed that could oil and renew its own parts, so as not to stop or break, or need repairing or oiling or cleaning, such a product would be more complex. But if, in addition to running on uninterruptedly for a long series of years, or almost an entire century, suppose it could be so constructed and constituted that, without interrupting the orderly movement of its works or its accuracy and correctness, it should, at intervals, produce other watches like itself. Truly such a watch would be a marvelous complexity. Yet just such a complexity is found in all the forms of vegetable and animal life about us. Interesting as is the study of life at any stage, it is specially interesting and impressive during the periods which preface, accomplish and follow the wonderful period of gestation; and it is specially important that the individual who stands so closely related to this profound and awe-inspiring mystery as does a young husband should have such knowledge of what this condition has to teach as comes within the realm of human understanding—both because of its importance to his own happiness, the happiness, safety and well-being of the mother and her offspring, and because such knowledge will tend to purify the mind of those gross and debasing thoughts which too frequently cluster about the most important and most sacred relations of married life and the endearments of home.

Something of what these changes are which precede, attend and follow reproduction in the human family may be beautifully seen in a conservatory or garden, or even learned from the frail flower that blooms by the roadside.

When, in the springtime or summer days, the plant has reached its maturity, as instinctively as if it foresaw in the coming days of autumn and in the ice and snow of winter the possibility not only of death but of total extinction, its entire nature centres in one grand struggle to escape pending extermination and live, if not in its own body, yet in the life and beauty that shall be reproduced in the plants that are already begotten in the longing for the perpetuity of its own life. The dual parent-nature is quickened. Forgetting the present, and longing for a place and a part when the warm and quickening breath of spring shall again usher in a new day of life and beauty upon the earth the plant henceforth lives, not for the present, but for the future; not for itself, but for those that are to be. The buds begin to form. The plant has learned the purpose of being and throbs with the mystery of life. In the thought of death it has learned to live. In fear of extinction it has learned to perpetuate and multiply itself a hundredfold. The flower unfolds. The dual parent-nature of the plant lives with intensity in their common effort. The flower is in a passion of beauty, in an agony of splendor, perfuming the nuptial hour with a sweetness that distills upon the air, arresting the hurrying steps of all who pass by. Who shall dare to interrupt that ceremonial, whose ruthless hand shall dare defeat that high and holy purpose? The fragrance invites the bees and insects to the nuptial feast. For them there is pollen and nectar in abundance. They bear gifts of quickening pollen from other plants, or swing the anther censers that waited the coming of expected guests. The corolla of beauty screens the enchanted participants. The ceremonial is over, the hour is ended. The ovules have felt the thrill of life, the beauty fades, the fragrance is gone, the wedding-garments are laid aside, and henceforth the father-nature and the mother-nature of the plant live not for themselves, but for the life they have begotten, and the plants that shall be. Their joy abides, and they live in the glad hope of participation, in the succeeding resurrection of the life and beauty and fragrance that is to await the coming of another springtime.

What we have written in allegory takes place in fact. Every intelligent observer has noted the depth of color, passionate beauty, and sweet fragrance of the flower as the hour approaches when the stigma awaits the pollen which is to fertilize the ovules that lie hidden away in the ovary or pod. When that union has been effected the flower fades, its petals fall off; the calyx, which as a vase held the corolla erect in its splendor, but which remains to shield and protect the ovules or little seeds which are being formed and perfected, now droops, turning toward the earth. Is this a sign of sadness, or that there is no longer any joy in life? No, no, not at all. It is the evidence of its fidelity to the sacred trust that has been committed to it. It has found a new joy, a more abiding happiness. Then it held up the corolla that the sun and the angels might look in upon the happy and holy beginnings of life, while now, in the protection of its sacred trust, it turns down, that it may shed the rain and everything that might intrude or hurt the tender plant that is so mysteriously encased in that pod that enlarges with the growing life that is within it.

What is true in the reproductive life of plants is also true in the reproductive life of man. The changes that take place at the moment of conception and during the period of gestation are full of marvelous beauty and profound mystery. The bright eyes, the ruby lips, the ruddy glow on the cheeks, the comely attire, the attractive manner, the persuasive sweetness, the subtle but indescribable attractiveness, are manifestations in human life of what may be seen and studied with such impressiveness in the reproductive life of the flower. The changes which follow may not be as immediate; and while, to the unknowing and unobservant, they may not at first be totally unobserved, yet to the devout student they are quite as manifest and pronounced as in the flowers; and the study of these changes which attend the beginning, the growth and the completion of reproduction is one of great interest to every intelligent person, although its clear presentation to those who have no knowledge whatever of the subject is attended with some difficulty.

As the birds at the mating season put on their most gorgeous plumage, sing their sweetest songs, and in the building of their nests work in sweetest accord, so it is also in human life. When the nest is completed, the eggs laid, and the incubation or hatching begins, the plumage soon loses some of its lustre, the songs become less frequent, and the parent birds prepare for the feeding and care of the bird-life that is soon to fill the nest.

But all this quickening of life and growth that takes place in the egg within the nest under the warm body of the mother-bird, in the human mother takes place within the nest or cradle which God has prepared within her body. Her young is of a higher order. The protection and preservation of the unfolding human life is more important, and hence the greater care displayed in guarding and nourishing it.

The future mother, whose nature only recently craved her husband's caresses and embraces, now, perhaps all unconsciously to herself, changes, to fit her for the better completion of the sacred and holy work which God has assigned her. The eye loses somewhat of its lustre, the cheek its ruddy glow, and her entire being something of that pervasive sweetness which but recently made her peculiarly attractive. But to the intelligent husband and true father she is none the less, but rather the more, an object of love and adoration ; and if she is intelligent, and understands the high and holy nature of that which is being wrought within her own body, and the exalted honor which God has bestowed upon her in making her a co-creator with himself, she will not manifest the belligerent and uncompanionable spirit which too often characterizes the bearing of some women during this period of unfolding life.

While it is true that the changes which accompany this period are more marked in woman than in man, yet when we remember that a close study of the reproductive nature of man in married life discloses a responsiveness to her condition and desires, it will readily be understood that during the period of his wife's gestation his nature is measurably moderated by her condition, for in health the reproductive nature of man is responsive to the promptings of his wife. The poet wisely says:

> "As unto the bow the cord is,
> So unto the man is woman.
> Though she bends him, she obeys him;
> Though she draws him, yet she follows—
> Useless each without the other."

Where existing facts in any particular case are discordant with this poetic figure the causes can usually be found in an abnormal passion in the man, or a measurable absence of sexual inclination in the woman, frequently caused by ruinous modes of life and dress. While human beings are generally very different in this respect from the lower animals, yet something of what these changes are may be suggested by noting the changes which take place in bird life. As the wave of life rises to its crest in the male nature, every department of his being is aroused to greatest activity and perfection. His plumage becomes lustrous, he sings with sweetest note. In some of the animals the intensity of his vitality bursts out in a growth of great antlers; but when the mating season is passed the plumage fades; the antlers drop off as the receding tide of life sets in. These marked changes among the animals are by no means paralleled in man; yet there are semblances or faint shadows of them in the modifying of the male nature.

While such external and manifest changes as we have indicated are taking place, marvelous things are being wrought within the mother's body. The ovum or egg (for that is what it truly is), after it has left the place where it matured in the ovary, is impregnated by the spermatozoön, which, in its restless search for the ovum, presses forward from the place where it was liberated in the vagina, up through the womb, and out through the Fallopian tube toward the ovary; or the ovum may pass through the Fallopian tube and into the womb, to await for a brief period or a few days the coming of the sperm or spermatozoön, without which it must remain incomplete and perish.

God might just as easily have ordained that the ovum should be complete in itself, and that, without any intervention or co-operation, at appointed intervals the mother should bring forth her offspring. But there were reasons why this should not be. The begetting and bringing forth of human life involves issues too vast to be committed to a single individual. Without a defender or protector during this period when the mother is rendered measurably helpless by her condition, would imperil the safety and even the life of both parent and child. Two must share the risks and the responsibilities. The father, during this period and that which follows, is to bear the burdens of life largely alone. He is to provide food and shelter. He is to be the guardian and the defender of his more dependent companion. Should exposure or peril result in the death of the mother, the child must not be left without a natural guardian and caretaker. This young life is too precious to be exposed to possible peril. Its care, its nurture, its education is too important even to be risked with a single parent. The mother might " forget her sucking child, that she should not have compassion on the son of her womb," and it was important that the child should then have another, who is bound by natural and moral obligations, and by bonds of personal interest and tenderest affection, to care for it. This double parentage gives the child four grandparents instead of two, and eight great-grandparents instead of four. In this wise way the child is knit to many in an obligation to nurture and care for it, should necessity arise. If physical, mental and moral infirmity should exist in the mother, the force of such infirmity must be reasonably broken by a new stream of influences which tend to liberate the child from any inheritance of incapacity. If the father is wicked or worthless, the child is to find its defender and caretaker in its mother;

or, should the mother possess these bad qualities, the child may find in its father its defense and help. The life and well-being of the child is so important that it must have two chances to be well-born and well-reared.

But this relation of interdependence is not only for the well-being of the offspring, but for the highest physical, intellectual and moral development and well-being of both parents. Parenthood comes not only to the mother, molding, fashioning and perfecting her in every department of her being, but when intelligently and reverently assumed, when discharged with fidelity and self-denial, it has its priceless endowments for the father as well. In view of the Creator's full and sacred purpose, who shall dare invade, or even lightly assume, the far-reaching responsibilities which God has united to parenthood? "What God hath joined together, let not man put asunder."

What intelligent man or woman shall dare trample under their feet all the sacred relations of life, and call into being an immortal spirit whose temporal and eternal destinies are to be affected by its advent into a world that is waiting to brand it because begotten of an illicit union? What husband or wife can regard with dishonor, or dare debase, the God-given powers of reproduction?

But to return to the subject of the changes which take place within the body of the mother during this period of wondrous interest. When the spermatozoa have been liberated in the upper portion of the vagina at the cervix, or small opening which forms what is called the neck of the womb, although such minute microscopic objects that when laid end to end it would require five hundred of them to make an inch in length, yet, with that wonderful activity of which we have written in a previous chapter, they immediately seek the doorway into the womb, that mysterious chamber where the ovum may naturally be expected to await their coming. We correctly think of persons, and not of things, as possessed of intelligence and acting in accordance with reason, but this mysterious natal chamber within the mother's body appears instinct with intelligence. It seems almost as though across its portals were written, in a language which every object and every spermatozoön might read, the prohibition: "None save those who bear the gift of life may enter or tarry within these portals." The ovum may remain for a period, and the spermatozoa that seek the ovum may enter, but neither may tarry unless each yields itself to the other in that mysterious union which results in life. Apart or alone, after a brief period, they must alike be cast out; no idler may tarry there; but that semblance to innate intelligence which rejects or casts out any incomplete part as a foreign substance accords a hearty welcome to the ovum that has been quickened into a new life by the entrance of a spermatozoön. No mother ever embraced her newborn child more lovingly, or regarded it with greater tenderness, than the womb receives the quickened ovum. When the ovum is quickened, every fibre of being thrills with a new purpose. A royal place is speedily prepared for the safety, nurture and development of the ovum. The entire nature of the mother now centres upon the accomplishment of a special work—that of developing and bringing forth the new life begotten within. Great changes are to be wrought not only in the ovum, but the enlarging life and new necessities are to be met by corresponding changes in the womb itself. Not only is the minute speck of life which is laid within this human cradle to develop into a fully-organized human being, but the cradle is to enlarge with the growth of its occupant, and respond to the varying needs of the unfolding and developing body within.

It will require the aid of a microscope to discover and observe the object of our search and study. The egg of the bird bears some proportion to the size of its producer, for in them is stored up the nourishment which is to maintain the unfolding life that can be fed in no other way until it has reached an advanced stage of maturity, and has broken its shell and emerged into the outer world. The human egg is so small that it would require two hundred and forty of them laid side by side to make one inch in length. They contain the nourishment which is to foster this minute beginning of human life for a brief period, after which it is to derive all its nourishment from the mother,

Her food is to furnish the material for its upbuilding. Its blood is to flow from her heart. The egg of the bird is encased in a porous covering through which pure air, with its transforming power, is to find its way to the developing life within; but this human egg and the life which it is designed to unfold must owe all to its mother. Her lungs must impart the oxygen it needs, and her body must minister to every function of the body of the child, until after a period of months, when it shall have reached that stage of development when it is prepared to enter upon its own independent life in the outer world.

This minute germ of human life, this egg so small that a thousand could be laid upon a ten-cent piece, this atom, which under the microscope shows a speck of oil and albumin, which in the course of a few brief months is to constitute a complex human organism, with all the perfected parts and wonderful adjustment of a human body, already contains the elements of a new human soul. Embodied in this undeveloped human germ is the future man or woman. Here are all the elements which are to make the successful mechanic, the farmer, the orator, or the statesman. Ingrained in these forming tissues may be scrofula, consumption or insanity. Here, already, are the inheritances which are to determine whether this being shall be temperate or intemperate, chaste or licentious. The moral nature has already received that bent which will incline it to reach out after God and heaven and holy things, or which will incline it downward to all that is base, destructive, and that tends to death. The history of this immortal being is already measurably outlined in the past life of the father and the mother. What they have been in their thought, in their character, in their being, that their child is largely to become. This outline is now subjected to modifications by the thought and life of the mother during the few months while the body of her child is being unfolded, fashioned and developed beneath and so close to her own heart. During these months, her life is to tell both upon the body and the soul of her child.

During the brief period while the germ within the fertilized egg is being nourished by the vitellus or yolk of the egg, great changes are taking place in the soft and delicate linings which surround it within the womb. While, of course, the greatest changes which take place during the period of gestation are chiefly within the ovum or egg, yet those which take place in the body of the mother herself are more manifest, and scarcely less marvelous. The mucous membrane within the walls of this enclosure begins to thicken; the small vessels which compose the structure of the inner surface begin to multiply, enlarge, and lengthen, until they are manifest to the unaided eye. This soft, velvety lining becomes thick and rich, but loses none of its softness and delicacy.

Every preparation is speedily made, and the fertilized egg finds lodgment in the thin, delicate folds of the membrane in the upper central portion or dome of the womb. The folds begin to grow about the egg, partially enclosing it, and shutting it off from the general cavity of the womb. At last the borders of this growing envelope meet, and form a complete and distinct enclosure. This thin, transparent tissue, which constitutes a living envelope or sac, shuts off the egg or growing embryo from the rest of the cavity of the womb, which its increasing proportions are soon completely to fill.

The original membranous lining which covers the entire interior of the womb, and which has now become thickened or tumefied, as medical men say, is technically called the decidua vera, while that portion of the membrane which forms the sac that surrounds and encloses the egg is called the decidua reflex. These are known as "decidua," which means "not permanent"—a word applied to those things in nature which after a period drop away, as leaves, teeth and horns, which are shed or fall off. So the decidua reflex is to pass away with the birth, and the decidua vera is to change back again into its normal condition.

The egg, which during this period has considerably enlarged, begins to throw out upon all sides threadlike tissues, by which this germ of life becomes attached to and grows into the mother-life upon which it is engrafted.

It is through these filaments that the fluids which are to nourish and develop this unfolding life are imparted from the mother and received by the embryo.

As the attachment between the sac which encloses the egg more firmly and securely adheres to the walls of the womb the filaments which had formed upon all sides of the enclosing sac begin to disappear, except upon the side in contact with the womb. Upon that side they become more pronounced, and in the third month the permanent attachment known as the placenta, through which the embryo is to receive its increasing supply of nourishment from the body of the mother, begins to be formed. The placenta is circular in shape, from one to two inches in thickness in its thickest part, and about six or eight inches in diameter. It forms the temporary medium of communication between the life of the mother and that of the child, and, properly speaking, is not a part of either. It is formed for a temporary use, which terminates with the birth of the child; and at that time the placenta, the umbilical or navel cord, and the membrane we have named, constitute what is called the afterbirth.

The placenta is a flat, soft disk which is attached to the walls of the womb connecting the embryo by the navel cord, through which it respires or breathes, and receives nourishment, and discharges the worn-out particles of matter. It is through this attachment or cord that an intimate connection is established between the growing life of the ovum and the currents of life which flow in the mother's body. Through this placentic cord the embryo receives oxygen and all the elements necessary for its growth, upon the one hand, while, upon the other, it also transfers to the body of the mother the carbonic acid gas and other impurities which in the process of life are necessary to be thrown off.

CHAPTER XV.

THE CHANGES WHICH PRECEDE, ATTEND AND FOLLOW CONCEPTION AND CHILDBIRTH.

Continued.

BUT while these changes have been taking place within the womb itself, and the decidua or thickened membrane has been forming about this developing germ of life, let us consider some of the changes which have taken place within the ovum itself. If observant when opening a hen's egg, the observer will notice that the yolk is covered by a very thin membrane which encloses and separates it from the other portion of the egg, and holds it in its rounded form. The membrane is exceedingly delicate, but sufficiently thick and strong to serve its intended purpose. Now, the human ovum or egg consists of a vitellus or yolk, which is covered by a similar membrane, known as the vitelline. When this ovum or egg has been fertilized or impregnated, remarkable changes take place. This vitellus or yolk undergoes a series of segmentation or dividings which are known as spontaneous segmentation. The single minute yolk divides itself into two smaller balls or segments. These again subdivide into four; these four subdivide into eight, the eight into sixteen, and so on, resulting in the rearrangement of the yolk into a finely divided granular mass. While this division is in process, the divided parts arrange themselves orderly about the inner surface of the vitelline or yolk membrane, with the minute microscopic spaces between filled with a transparent fluid. While these cells have been multiplying and become so abundant as to be flattened against the internal surface of the yolk membrane, they have developed into true animal cells. The edges of these cells, where they come in contact with each other, form a continuous organized membrane, which lies just within the yolk membrane. This membrane is called the blastodermic membrane.

This new membrane, formed within the sac which originally enclosed the yolk of the ovum, now divides or separates itself into two distinct layers, known as the outer and inner blastodermic membranes, also called epiblast and hypoblast. The egg at this stage of development presents the appearance of a small round sac, the walls of which consist of three layers, each succeeding layer lying immediately within and in contact with the other which encloses it. The outer one of the three is the primitive yolk sac, the second is the outer layer of the blastodermic membrane, and the third the inner layer, while the interior cavity of the egg is filled by the transparent fluid previously mentioned.

In order to understand the beginnings of life it is important to have a clear conception of these different sacs, for these two membranes lying within the yolk sac, and together known as the blastodermic membrane, and separately as the outer and inner layers of the blastodermic membrane, contain the anatomical elements from which the organized being with its fully-formed body is to grow. Indeed, it may be said that these two blastodermic membranes are the body of the embryo which is to develop into the fully-formed physical man.

The noting of this division into two separate layers is important, for the outer one develops into the skin, spinal cord, muscles and bone, while from the inner layer is formed the intestinal canal and the organs of vegetative life.

Between these two blastodermic membranes other minute tissues are formed, the office and end of which are not so fully understood, and the consideration of which would lead us into intricacies beyond our present purpose.

The first visible sign of the organic structure of the human form is discovered as it takes shape upon the exterior wall of the blastodermic membrane, known as the embryonic spot, and known also as the primitive trace or furrow. It is supposed that from this is formed the spinal canal, with the dorsal plate upon either side, from which springs the framework of the bony structure, and at one end of which is the large rounded cavity which forms the receptacle for the brain and the medulla oblongata, or the upper cranial portion of the spinal cord, which is to control respiration, and at the other extremity of which, in a later stage, will sprout or grow the legs and feet.

Without complicating the subject too much for the clear understanding of the ordinary reader by undertaking to explain minute changes which are very interesting to specialists, but likely to detract from its interest and value to the ordinary reader, let it suffice to say that in the course of a brief period the embryo which has grown mainly from the two blastodermic membranes which we have described, and is attached to the walls of the womb by the placenta and cord which carries the blood and life-currents from the body of the mother to the growing body of the child within, is at this period of its development surrounded and enclosed by a number of membranes. The outer one of these is the inner lining of the womb itself, known as the decidua vera. Within this is the decidua reflex, the membrane of the womb, which extended itself and grew around the ovum, completely enclosing it. The third is the chorion, forming the outer membrane which encloses the fetus, and within which is the amnion, or innermost membrane which surrounds the fetus, and between which is another membrane, called the allantois.

The amnion, which is the innermost of the membranes surrounding the fetus, seemingly has a special office, which is to secrete the fluid technically called the amniotic. This fluid is popularly known as "the waters." This secretion performs several important offices. It protects the fetus from any local pressure or blow, and so distributes any pressure as to enable all the parts to grow without danger of distortion and deformity. It also affords the fetus greater freedom of motion, and protects the womb and other parts from injuries which might otherwise be inflicted by the fetus after quickening. Within this fluid the fetus floats during its formative period, and when the time of birth comes the breaking of the sac which contains this fluid enables it to flow out, lubricating the parts, or channel, through which the newly formed being is to pass in its exit into the outer world. The importance of this fluid in this latter office is of great moment. When the sac breaks and the waters flow away too much in advance of the birth of the child, there generally occur the inconveniences that attend what is called a "dry birth."

As already mentioned in a previous paragraph, during the first weeks of growth the embryo is nourished the same as the young chick within the egg, by the yolk, in which its earliest nourishment has been stored.

Soon the delicate union is formed between the chorion by the gathering and multiplication of the villi or minute hair-like membranes, which gather into a compact mass and adhere to the adjacent portion of the womb. This formation is known as the placenta, previously described, which is constituted of two portions—the maternal side, which is toward the walls of the womb, and the fetal side, which is toward the growing fetus. Upon the inner side, the placenta is united with the fetus by two arteries which are wrapped around the one vein, which together unite with the body of the placenta. Through these the life-currents flow; and, while the circulation between the bodies of mother and child are not direct or uninterrupted, for the fetus has its own measurably independent circulation, yet from the time the connection is formed until the cord is severed at birth the fetus derives all its nourishment from the mother.

Let us turn now to note the rapid changes which take place within the germ or egg from the time of its impregnation to the hour of the birth of the child. The changes, although seemingly very minute at first, are nevertheless very rapid from the beginning to the period of maturity and birth. The following account, taken from " Plain Talks on Avoided Subjects," by Henry N. Guernsey, M.D., constitutes a goodly portion of the introductory chapter of that excellent little book, and presents the matter in the intelligible and impressive manner we desire for this place, and is quoted in full by permission:

" The first indication of formation that is possible to discover, even by the help of the microscope, consists of an oblong figure, obtuse at one extremity, swollen in the middle, blunt-pointed at the other extremity. The rudimen tary embryo is slightly curved forward, is of a grayish-white color, of a gelatinous consistence, from two to four lines long, and weighs one or two grains. A slight depression, representing the neck, enables us to distinguish the head; the body is marked by a swollen centre, but there are as yet no traces of the extremities. So much can be observed about the end of the third week after conception.

"At about the *fifth week* the embryo presents more distinctions. The head is very large in proportion to the rest of the body, the eyes are represented by two black spots, and the upper extremities by small protuberances on the sides of the trunk. The embryo at this stage is nearly two-thirds of an inch in length and weighs about fifteen grains. The lower extremities now begin to appear in the shape of two minute rounded tubercles. Till about this time a straight artery has been observed to beat with the regularity of the pulse; but now it appears doubled somewhat into the shape of an adult heart, although as yet it has but one auricle and one ventricle. As time advances we find the perfect heart, with its two ventricles and two auricles, all developed from the original straight artery. At this period the lungs appear to exist in five or six different lobes, and we can barely distinguish the bronchial tubes; about the same time the ears and face are distinctly outlined, and after awhile the nose is also faintly and imperfectly perceived.

"At about the *seventh week* : little bony deposit is found in the lower jaw. The kidneys now begin to be formed, and a little later the genital organs. The embryo averages one inch in length.

"At *two months* the rudiments of the extremities become more prominent. The forearm and hand can be distinguished, but not the arm above the elbow; the hand is larger than the forearm, but is not supplied with fingers. The sex cannot yet be determined. The length of the embryo is from one inch and a half to two inches, and it weighs from three to five drachms. The eyes are discernible, but still uncovered by the rudimentary lids. The nose forms an obtuse eminence, the nostrils are rounded and separated, the mouth is gaping, and the epidermis can be distinguished from the true skin.

"At *ten weeks* the embryo is from one and a half to two and a half inches long, and its weight is from one ounce to an ounce and a half; the eyelids are more developed, and descend in front of the eyes; the mouth begins to be closed by the development of the lips. The walls of the chest are more completely formed, so that it is no longer possible to see the movements of the heart. The fingers become distinct, and the toes appear as small projections webbed together like a frog's foot. At about this period the sexual organs show their development, as follows: On each side of the urinary locality an oblong fold becomes distinguishable; in course of progress, if these folds remain separate, a little tubercle forms in the anterior commissure which becomes the clitoris; the nymphæ develop, the urethra forms between them, and the female sex is determined. If, on the other hand, these folds unite into a rounded projection, the scrotum is formed, the little tubercle above becomes the penis, and hence the male sex. The testicles forming within the body descend later into the scrotum, and organs similar to them, their counterparts, form in the females and are called ovaries. These ovaries are found attached to an organ called the womb, and this, again, is united with the vagina, which leads downwards and outwards between the labia majora (or larger lips).

"At the end of the *third month* the weight of the embryo is from three to four ounces and its length from four to five inches; the eyeballs are seen through the lids, the pupils of the eyes are discernible, the forehead, nose and lips can be clearly distinguished. The finger-nails resemble thin membranous plates, the skin shows more firmness, but is still rosy-hued, thin and transparent. The sex can now be fully determined.

"At the end of the *fourth month* the product of conception is no longer called an embryo, but a fetus. The body is from six to eight inches in length, and weighs six or seven ounces. A few little white hairs are seen scattered over the scalp. The development of the face is still imperfect. The eyes are now closed by their lids, the nostrils are well-formed, the mouth is shut in by the lips, and the sex is still more sharply defined. The tongue may be observed far back in the mouth, and the lower part of the face is rounded off by what a little later will be a well-formed chin. The movements of the fetus are by this time plainly felt by the mother, and if born at this time it may live several months.

"At the end of the *fifth month* the body of the fetus is from seven to nine inches long, and weighs from eight to eleven ounces. The skin has a fairer appearance and more consistence; the eyes can no longer be distinguished through the lids, owing to the increased thickness of the latter. The head, heart and kidneys are large and well-developed.

"At the end of the *sixth month* the fetus is from eleven to twelve and a half inches in length, and weighs about sixteen ounces, more or less. The hair upon the scalp is thicker and longer, the eyes remain closed, and very delicate hairs may be seen upon the margins of the eyelids and upon the eyebrows. The nails are solid, the scrotum small and empty, the surface of the skin appears wrinkled, but the dermis may be distinguished from the epidermis. The liver is large and red, and the gall-bladder contains fluid.

"At the end of the *seventh month* the length of the fetus is from twelve and a half to fourteen inches; its weight is about fifty-five ounces, and it is both well-defined and well-proportioned in all its parts. The bones of the cranium, hitherto quite flat, now appear a little arched, and, as the process of ossification goes on, the arching increases until the vault is quite complete. The brain presents greater firmness, and the eyelids are opened. The skin is much firmer, and red. The gall-bladder contains bile.

"At the end of the *eighth month* the fetus seems to thicken up rather than to increase in length, since it is only from sixteen to eighteen inches long, while its weight increases from four to five pounds. The skin is red, and characterized at this period by a fine downy covering, over which is spread a quantity of thick viscous matter, called the sebaceous coat, which has been forming since the latter part of the fifth month. The lower jaw has now become as long as the upper one, and in the male the left testicle may be found in the scrotum. Convolutions appear in the brain structure.

"At *nine months* the anxious time of parturition (or birth) has arrived. The fetus is from nineteen to twenty-three inches in length, and weighs on an average from six to eight pounds. Children at birth sometimes weigh as much as fourteen pounds; but such extremes are very rare. At this period the white and gray matter of the brain are distinct, and the convolutions are well marked; the nails assume a horny consistence, hair upon the head is more or less abundant, the testes are in the scrotum, and the entire external genital organs of both male and female are well formed.

How wonderfully and how instructively are all organs in the animal body disposed and arranged! In the highest place we find the brain to govern and rule over all below. It is the first organ formed, and in an orderly life should control all the others. Next in order and importance are the heart and lungs, which put into motion all other parts and enable the animal frame to continue in motion. So each and every organ is developed in its proper order, all to obey the commands of the first and most important—the brain, the seat of the reason and the will. Happy are they of either sex who will govern themselves by a pure, enlightened reason and a pure, affectionate will."

While we may note the various stages of change and progress, yet to the thoughtful student there lies back of all these outer manifestations a hidden life, a divine unfolding of the human body which is mysterious and awe-inspiring. While we know something of what takes place, yet the declaration of the Book of Ecclesiastes is impressively true: "Thou knowest not what is the way of the Spirit, nor how the bones do grow in the womb of her that is with child." All who study it thoughtfully and reverently can exclaim with David: "I am fearfully and wonderfully made: marvelous are Thy works; and that my soul knoweth right well. My substance was not hid from Thee, when I was made in secret, and curiously wrought in the lowest parts of the earth. Thine eyes did see my substance, yet being imperfect; and in Thy book all my members were written, which in continuance were fashioned, when as yet there was none of them."

Let us turn now to the mother who has nourished and who is about to bring into the world the body of an immortal being. Some of the changes most easily noted in the body of the mother occur as she reaches the period when approaching maturity has prepared the body of the child for an early entrance into the outer world. Marvelous as are the less noticeable changes which have earlier taken place, the time has now come when others which are more marked are soon to manifest themselves. Several days prior to the event there is a dropping or subsidence of the womb. This is preparatory to the distention and enlargement of the vagina through which the exit is to be made. The stomach and lungs are relieved of pressure, the mother feels more easy, is more inclined to move about, breathes more freely, and the sense of oppression which formerly caused her to desire inaction passes away, and Providence thus fits her to make such necessary preparations as are important in view of the event which is soon to take place. As the days approach, the external parts give indication of the distention and enlargement which has taken place in the vagina and the preparations which nature is making for the more easy exit of the life which has developed within.

The entire physical nature of the mother is in a state of preparation for the great event. A large quantity of blood is being sent to the breasts, the lacteals are developing, and the preparation is being completed for the secretion of milk, so that there may be no lack when the little stranger arrives.

One of the earliest indications that the event is about to take place is the discharge of the small plug of mucus which has served to hermetically seal the neck of the womb against the entrance of any foreign substance; but its office or work is now completed. The cervix, or neck of the womb, enlarges, and this little plug, popularly known as "the show," passes away with some streaks of blood. While the neck of the womb, the vaginal passage and the external parts have greatly enlarged, the womb itself is beginning to contract preparatory to the expulsion of that which it has fostered and nourished for a period of about nine months.

The earliest premonition that these contractions are taking place is found in the grinding pains, which come at irregular intervals, sometimes a couple of hours apart, or only separated by a half hour, or even a shorter period. These contractions of the abdominal muscles are soon followed by the true labor-pains, which come at more regular intervals. These grinding pains are felt in the back and loins. The contractions rise to a certain pitch of intensity, and then as gradually abate. Usually, as the regular labor-pains begin, the fluid contained in the amniotic sac, and within which the child has floated during its period of growth, is now liberated by the breaking of the sac, flows through the vaginal passage, lubricating the parts and preparing all for an easy exit of the body of the infant into the outer world. When the presentation is normal the head comes first, and usually in a period varying from a few minutes to a few hours the child is born. In exceptional cases the labor may be extended over a day or more, but such cases are relatively rare.

The apprehensions of dangers which associate themselves in the minds of many with childbirth are not often realized. If the parts are not diseased, and the mother is in good health, and the laws of the unfolding life have been carefully observed, there is little peril, although, generally, considerable pain. There are many physicians who have attended hundreds of women in confinement who have never lost but an exceptional case or two. The extreme pain endured by many women is largely due to the lack of that knowledge which would have enabled the mother to approach this period with but little apprehension, and to have passed through the period of parturition or childbirth with but slight inconvenience and pain.

While the perils may be greatly reduced and the pains greatly diminished, it is nevertheless a period of wonderful revolution throughout the entire physical nature of the mother. The blood which flowed from her heart to nourish and foster the growing body of her child is now turned in other directions, and the fountains at which the child is to receive its food and its strength begin to flow with their richness of life-giving currents.

After the placenta and the sacs which enclosed the fetus, which together constitute what is known as "the afterbirth," have passed away, the recuperating and renewing powers with which God has so wonderfully endowed the body of the mother beyond that of the father become active. The muscular tissues of the womb, vagina and the external parts at once begin to contract, and the entire nature of the mother begins to adjust itself to the new relations of her child to her own body and the necessities of nourishing and guarding it upon the external portion of her body, rather than within that mysterious chamber which God prepared for its beginning and the earliest unfoldings of its infant life.

When the child is born into the world its body also undergoes a wonderful revolution. Then, for the first time, its heart takes up its own independent action; air for the first time enters the cells of the lungs, and with the early shock, if it might so be called, of taking its first breath, the child usually utters its first cries. During the period of its fetal life the lungs have received only so much blood as was necessary for their own growth and development, but with the first breath they expand and receive the inflowing of the blood from the right side of the heart. This involves the opening of some passages and the closing of others. These are but the first of a series of transformations which are early to take place. The various veins, arteries and ducts which have hitherto received the supplies of blood from the placenta and returned the worn and wasted material to that same centre, or distribute the supplies for special service throughout different portions of the body, by the cutting of the umbilical or navel cord, and the separation of the child from the placenta and body of the mother, now assume a new relation to the independent body of the newborn child. Some of these ducts and arteries soon entirely close, and in some instances degenerate into impervious cords with new and important offices; some are transformed into true ligaments, while others remain pervious. Now that the primitive purposes of some of these parts have been fulfilled, the parts themselves disappear, while still other parts take upon themselves new offices and duties which are imposed by the changes incident to birth—the separation from the body of the mother and the entrance upon its own independent life in the outer world.

Truly, "we are fearfully and wonderfully made." The infinite Author of all things has left the stamp of His wisdom upon everything that He has created. Whether we take the microscope and study the earliest beginnings and mysterious unfoldings of this spark of human life; whether we study the blade of grass beneath our feet, or the stars that shine over our heads; everywhere we find the wonderful wisdom of our Creator. "Day unto day uttereth speech, and night unto night showeth knowledge." It matters not whether we listen to the lessons of a flower, the history of an atom, or the song of the spheres, "there is no speech nor language where their voice is not heard; their line is gone out through all the earth, and their words to the end of the world."

CHAPTER XVI.

WHEN THE BABY IS BORN.

At the end of about 280 days after the conception, or what under ordinary conditions would have been the tenth menstrual period, the days are completed and the expectant mother is usually delivered of her child. The day when the indications are that the child is to be born is always one of great anxiety, but need not be one of apprehension or fear. Where the laws of health have been observed there is no cause for apprehension. With the birth of the first child the labor is oftentimes somewhat more prolonged and attended with more pain, but the after-pains are usually not considerable. Generally the pains which precede the birth diminish with each succeeding confinement, but the after-pains increase in a similar manner.

Where the mother has made intelligent preparation for this great event, the child may be, and generally is, born without the actual assistance of the doctor. An intelligent nurse would be in position to render every needed assistance, but the presence of a well-equipped physician always brings such added ease to the mind of the mother, by removing all unnecessary risks, that it is always desirable that the physician should have been apprised in advance, notified promptly, and be on hand as soon as possible after the labor-pains commence. This is especially important when it is the first child.

If the labor should be short and the birth take place before the arrival of the physician, the nurse or attendant should be careful to see that the cord is not wound about the neck of the child, but placed free, and the child with its head in position so that it can breathe naturally, and with its body warmly covered.

When the pulsing in the cord has ceased and the child has cried vigorously, any nurse who has been present at previous confinements, who is intelligent and capable, would be able to sever the cord after having made the necessary bindings upon it. Indeed, some authorities contend that when the pulsing has *ceased* the cord may be severed without any tying of the ends at all.

Dr. Alice B. Stockham, in "Tokology," makes the following sensible suggestions: "Usually, as the child is ushered into the world, it sets up a lusty cry, indicating that respiration is established. Crying is not essential, as some authors claim, and the prompt covering usually causes it to desist. If it does not breathe at once, a little brisk patting on the breast and thigh may establish respiration. If this is not effectual, dash cold water in the face and on the chest. Still failing, artificial respiration must be established. To do this, close the nostrils with two fingers, blow into the mouth, and then expel the air from the lungs by a gentle pressure upon the chest. Continue this as long as any hope of life remains.

"*Sever the cord when pulsation has entirely ceased.* Use a dull pair of scissors, cutting about two inches from the child's navel. Following these directions, no tying is essential."

Tying is done in order to prevent excessive bleeding; but whether to tie the ends of the severed placentic cord, or not, is a matter which should be left wholly to the attendant doctor. It is well for the young husband to be intelligent and well-read along these and kindred lines, but if he employs a physician he should accept the physician's judgment and have his instructions followed. If he is not satisfied with the doctor whom he has employed, but sees fit to change for one whose opinions harmonize more closely with his own, that is a matter for the husband's own judgment, but the physician who is employed should always be supreme and left without interference or dictation. The doctor in charge must have absolute control in a lying-in room. He should direct, and not be dictated to.

If the husband is intelligent, enters into the sympathies of his wife, and has her confidence, if the physician consents, as he doubtless will, it seems quite natural that he should desire to be present with his wife in this trying experience of her life. If he understands the nature of the experience through which she is called upon to pass, his sympathy will be helpful to his wife, and if nature has endowed him with any of the qualifications of a good nurse, he can be of assistance to the doctor. Where the husband is without intelligence, is nervous, and exerts a depressing influence upon his wife, his absence may be more helpful than his presence. If the husband is intelligent and sympathetic, it seems to us that he could not but desire to be with his wife; but where he is wholly disqualified, his physician should not hesitate to express his judgment and preference in this matter.

The presence of a physician is always to be preferred, in order to determine the presentation, sever the cord, and look carefully after the afterbirth. The normal presentation is of the head foremost.

Where the inexperienced young husband is in an extremity, and finds himself alone at the hour of delivery, he should expect, as is most likely, that everything will move along normally, and he needs to be especially guarded only upon three points. When the head is born, see that the navel cord is not twisted around the child's neck. If this should be the case, it can easily be slightly loosened and then slipped over the child's head; otherwise the pressure of this tightened ligature would prevent its breathing and would result in strangulation. In an *extreme* case the cord could easily be tied in two places, a couple of inches apart, and cut between them. This should be done by an experienced person only, and as a last resort. After the child is born, the next and last important thing is the coming away of the placenta, or afterbirth. This often occurs at the end of twenty minutes or a half hour, or may be longer delayed. In the meantime the mother should be warmly covered, and any drink given her should not be either extremely hot or extremely cold. The afterbirth should be kept in a vessel prepared for it until the doctor has inspected it, so that he may know whether all the parts have come away or not. If any part remains, it might cause serious trouble.

These things successfully accomplished, the bathing of the child and care of the mother are next in order. How soon these should be undertaken would have to be determined by conditions. With the mother, a period of rest is sometimes very desirable. When bathing her body, or changing her bed, the greatest care should be exercised to protect her from the danger of contracting cold. During these hours her physical nature undergoes a great revolution, and exposure at this time might entail permanent results of a serious character. Fevers, bealed breasts, the aches, pains and perils which so often accompany and follow confinement, are almost wholly due to lack of proper care at this period.

If the young husband is intelligent and desires the comfort and well-being of his wife he will see that for a sufficient period she is protected against callers, and even the visits of friends. She is weak and needs absolute rest. She needs at least several days or more before she should be visited. If callers are allowed in her room, they are liable to remain too long. If you lack the nerve to decline callers the privilege they may expect, then ask your physician to order that no one see her at present.

The comfort, safety and well-being of the wife renders the selection of a good nurse a matter of as great importance as the choice of a good physician. In this matter the doctor is oftentimes the best counselor. He is constantly coming in contact with those who are in charge, where he is in attendance, and his suggestions ought to be most valuable. It is of the utmost importance that she should be a woman of pure blood; and for this a good moral character is the best guarantee. It is not wise to suppose that, since she is to remain but for a few weeks, the question of character is of no moment, for, without any outward evidences to arouse suspicion, she might bring with her, and by kissing and in other ways communicate to the child the results of venereal and other diseases which might entail, from this unsuspected source, consequences from which years could not bring subsequent relief.

Medical authorities assert that at least six weeks are required after childbirth before the womb assumes its natural size and position. An eminent physician, writing in the New York *Medical Journal*, says: "I have watched this very carefully in a number of women, and have seen in the perfectly clean womb of a non-nursing mother involution delayed as late as the third month."

It is perfectly safe to say that parents will make no mistake by observing the requirement of the Levitical teaching upon this subject.

After confinement or miscarriage, marital relations should be wholly omitted for a period. Upon this point the sanitary regulations of the Mosaic economy were very explicit. In the twelfth chapter of Leviticus instruction is given that after the birth of a male child at least forty days should elapse, and after the birth of a female, or maid child, at least eighty days should be permitted to elapse. Just why there should be this difference in time, six weeks after the birth of a male child and three months after the birth of a female child, seems not to be clearly understood either by theologians or medical authorities. When we know that this is intended and enjoined, we can rest assured that there are good and sufficient reasons, whether they be physical, social, sanitary or political.

No thoughtful or considerate husband would desire to impose upon his wife such exactions as would result in her certain discomfort, and possibly in such permanent physical injuries as are quite sure to follow.

One of the medical journals recently contained an incident narrated by a physician who had attended a woman in five different confinements. In each instance the physician noticed that about the seventh or eighth day the temperature of the patient indicated some unusual physical disturbance or irregularity. In the last confinement, when the physician called to mind similar conditions during previous periods of convalescence, he decided to discover the cause, and, by questioning the patient very critically, learned that the guilty husband was the occasion of his wife's trouble. While such occurrences are shameful in the highest degree, yet it is possible that such gross conduct is the occasion of many relapses upon the part of convalescing mothers, and to this it is probable that many deaths may easily be attributable.

That some husbands are brutal in this respect, we need but simply to name that an eminent physician of Philadelphia has stated that a legal friend had told him that he had procured a divorce within two years from her marriage for a wife whose charges of cruelty were sustained by the evidence that three days after her confinement her husband had driven the nurse out of his wife's room in order that he might make this cruel exaction of her.

After the little stranger is safely landed, bathed, dressed, and has had a sufficient period of rest, the matter of nourishment is likely to come up for consideration. The food which nature has provided is best suited to the physical requirements of the child, and is found in the mother's breasts. The earliest secretions of her breast constitute what is called colostrum, and is purgative in character, designed to cleanse the child's bowels of the meconium, or tar-like substance, with which they are filled previous to birth. Other food should never be substituted until failure has resulted in an honest, serious effort to conform to nature's purpose. If for any reason the child cannot obtain the nourishment which should be provided by the mother, it needs very little food until the third day.

If the serious results attendant upon artificial food and the provision of wet-nurses were fully understood, the terrible consequences which come to both the children and their parents, as the result of such courses, would be studiously avoided. The desire to escape the nursing and care of children, so as early to return to the rounds of social duties and marital excesses, is a great mistake. The well-being of the mother, as well as of the child, is dependent upon the fulfillment of the natural obligations which are inseparable from the relation of motherhood.

In large cities there are women who lead dissolute lives, put away their own children, and then rent themselves out as wet-nurses. When interviewed they tell plausible stories, and ingratiate themselves sometimes into good families, to render the double service of nurse and artificial mother. Many of these women are not only devoid of moral character, but bring to the child the degenerating influences which are inseparable from the vice and impurity which is a part of their own being. Not infrequently these women bring with them the after-effects of gonorrhea and syphilis, and the innocent child, which is entitled to the nourishment from the body of its own mother, is subjected by unthinking parents to the necessity of feeding at fountains which flow with corruption, disease and death.

It is on this very account that the children of the middle and even lower classes are generally stronger physically, intellectually and morally, than the children of those whose wealth and inclination incline them to dissipation and excess, to late hours and rich food, and who from simple preference subject their children to artificial food, or to the dangers and diseases which are so often brought into the home by a wet-nurse and vicious nurse-girls.

Fatherhood, no less than motherhood, has its duties and its pleasures. It is not only the father's duty, but it ought also to be his pleasure, to look after his own children. Some husbands speak of "the baby" as though it belonged wholly to the wife, and not to them. The thought of caring for or tending the child seems to be as foreign to their minds as though it were a child adopted by their wives from a foundling asylum.

It is not only the privilege, but the honor of the father to be found enjoying the pleasure and satisfaction of holding and caring for his children at proper times and intervals of leisure.

One of the prettiest pictures of home life is a painting in one of the galleries of Europe of the king of Belgium, upon his hands and knees upon the floor of the nursery, playing horse with his own royal children.

Some men seem to act as though it were a disgrace for them to carry their own children through the streets, or push the baby carriage when accompanied by their own wives. Every person has seen some strong, stalwart father, with weak character, walking by the side of a delicate, nervous wife, who is weak and faint because of the burden of carrying a child which belongs as much to the father as to the mother. Before they were married this same man would not allow the delicate darling by his side to carry her parasol; but now that they are married she is permitted to carry a child that weighs ten or twenty pounds, or even more, for great distances, because of the false pride of her unthoughtful husband.

We once knew a pastor of a prominent city church who lived adjacent to a small park where he was accustomed, at times, to sit in the shade and read. After a baby came into their home, being a sensible man, he found pleasure in giving some time and attention to his child; used sometimes to wheel it through the park in a baby carriage, or have the carriage stand near him while he sat and read. His home was not without a sufficient number of helpers, and one of his parishioners ventured one day to suggest that it was not becoming to take the baby with him when he went into the park to read; but the sensible father resented not only the insult which was offered to him personally, but to universal fatherhood, by replying that it was his baby, and he would do with it as he pleased.

The presence of a baby is a blessing in any home. It is a blessing to the father as well as to the mother. Some men are not good fathers, the same as some women are not the best of mothers; but any thoughtful husband will concede the fact that a proper apprehension of the relation which he sustains to the baby that is born in his home calls for a recognition of the privileges and obligations of a father to himself, to his child, and to his wife as well. What his home is, what his children are to become, will depend as much, and possibly more, upon what he is and does, than upon the little woman whose time, talent and strength are already taxed to their utmost by the various and constant demands which she must hourly meet.

Part III
CONCERNING HIS CHILDREN

CHAPTER XVII.

HEREDITY.

We now come in the third and last part of this book to write of what a young husband ought to know with regard to his children. If his children are to be greatly benefited by the wisdom of the father, he should be in possession of the knowledge imparted in the following chapters many years before he is in possession of the children. After they have received their inheritance from the parents, their bodies have been molded and fashioned, and bent and direction already given to their character, it is then too late to put such knowledge into practical use.

Much of what might be said in the closing chapters of this book has already found expression in the pages preceding. The doctrine of transmission and inheritance pervades not only this entire book, but also the two which precede it in the series. While it is true that too much importance cannot be placed upon the subject of heredity, the inheritance which we receive not only from our parents and grandparents but even from our great-grandparents, and while it is true that all that can be acquired in character and culture, both intellectual and physical, is transmitted from the parents to their children; yet possibly that which is by far the largest factor in determining the physical, intellectual, social and moral endowment of the child are found in the influences which mold and fashion the child during the months which lie between the period of conception and the time of birth. The potent influences of these different periods stand related to each other somewhat like what may be seen in the studio of an artist who molds and fashions in clay the models which are afterward to be actualized in brass or bronze. While the success of the work might be said to be greatly dependent upon the character, quality and condition of the clay brought to hand for this service, and while no perfect result could be secured with indifferent material, yet it is easy to see how, with the very best material at hand, an indifferent artist or a good artist when in indifferent mood would produce a very inferior model. If, with the thought of modifying the bronze figure after it has been cast, the artist is indifferent to the merits of the model which he is making, the final result can only prove a failure. No step in the work is unimportant, but the most important of all is the perfection of the model. In his hands the clay readily yields itself to his thought and impression; constant momentary care will prevent defects and deformities which could not be wholly remedied or refashioned, even by months and years of subsequent toil.

A wise man, when asked at what period a child's education should begin, replied:

"Twenty years before it is born." This is not an extreme statement, and if it errs in anything it errs in making the period too short rather than too long. Henry Ward Beecher once said that since so much depends upon one's ancestors, a man ought to be very careful in choosing his grandparents; and there is a vast deal of truth suggested by this statement. A young woman cannot be too careful in choosing the man who is to become the father of her children, and a young man cannot exercise too much care in selecting the woman who is to become the mother of his children.

In writing of heredity and prenatal influences, the subject divides itself naturally into the three periods which we have previously suggested— the preparation which precedes conception, the mental and physical condition at the time of conjunction, the environment and the mental and physical states of the mother during the period of gestation.

So much depends upon heredity that men who are interested in the breeding of horses for the race-course recognize the fact that unless a horse comes of racing stock he cannot be possessed of these essential qualities, without which he cannot possibly win. It is said by those who have made a study of it, that in England no horse has been known to win in any considerable race that was not bred of racing stock. Occasionally a horse with an ordinary pedigree may exhibit wonderful speed for a *short* distance, but none possesses the wind and endurance necessary for a long race with animals of a pure blood and a good pedigree. To this good inheritance the horseman adds constant training and the best of care. If these are at any time neglected, the horse begins to degenerate and reverts to the level of the ordinary animal.

It is generally agreed by physicians and those who have devoted time to the study of this subject that the mind and temper of the parents at the moment of conjunction have a great influence upon the temper and disposition of the child. Children should never be begotten except at those times when the husband and the wife can both bring their contribution of good health, affection and mental composure. Something of the effects produced by the mental states will appear by what we have to say in subsequent paragraphs.

In most instances it is perhaps true, as we have already suggested, that the greatest influences exerted upon the health, disposition and character are those which are effected by the physical and mental condition of the mother and the character of her environment during the period of gestation. While much of what we would like to know concerning prenatal influences is shrouded in mystery behind a veil that shuts us out from this holy of holies in which God dwells in mysterious creative power, yet we do know that peace of mind, equanimity of temper, purity of life, loving affections and exalted aspirations beget influences which are favorable to the production of the best physical, intellectual and moral endowments. If strong mental excitement, anger, emotion or fatigue affect injuriously the milk of the mother, so that the nursing child at once feels disturbed and injured, then we can reasonably understand how the child during the months prior to its birth, while it is even more dependent and far more intimately connected with the life-currents of the mother's body, and under the impress of her mental state, must be affected in a manner correspondingly greater.

While scientists at the present stage of inquiry and investigation have not been able to weigh and measure the force and effect of these influences, yet some results have been secured which help us to understand the existence of powers which were previously too subtle to be brought into the realm of human knowledge.

Something of the manner in which the mental condition of the mother may affect the child is suggested by the interesting experiments conducted by Prof. Elmer Gates in his laboratory at Chevy Chase, Washington, D. C. Prof. Gates has demonstrated the fact that even the breath is so affected by the mental state that by analyzing the residuum which remains upon a looking-glass which has been breathed upon, he is able to determine the character of the mental condition of the individual at the time the breath was exhaled upon the glass. Anger, revenge, jealousy, joy, pain, pleasure, and possibly all the emotions, stamp their distinctive messages upon the breath with as much accuracy as the little machine in the telegraph office registers its message in characters which we need only to know in order to be read. What some of these many characters are, Prof. Gates has been able to decipher, and his investigations and discoveries establish the fact that the mentality of the individual is stamped upon the breath.

The mind not only affects the breath, but it affects the entire individual; and this statement is proven by the fact that the character of the exhalations of the body are affected by the mentality of the individual. It is a well-known fact that not only does each different disease produce its own peculiar bodily odor, but mental states produce similar effects. It is affirmed that the odor in an insane asylum differs from the odor in all other institutions. It is stated that no amount of care and cleanliness, or even fumigation, can rid the wards and rooms of this subtle and distinctive odor, peculiar to the bodily exhalations of those who are affected with mental infirmities.

Insane asylums do not afford the only illustration. Institutions in which convicts are confined also have an odor which is distinctive. It differs from that of any other institution, and from the day that the buildings are completed and the convicts enter, the penitentiary odor is present, because inseparable from those who inhabit its wards. What is true of insane asylums and penitentiaries is doubtless true in a less pronounced manner of all institutions where persons are classified according to mental differences.

If the mental states of the mother affect her own bodily health, and if each of the diseases of the body and of the mind begets exhalations with distinguishing characteristics, it is easy to understand that the subtle effects of different mental states pervade the entire body. If these influences effect results beyond and without our own bodies, much more may they be expected to influence the unfolding mind and the developing body which are forming within the maternal body, and whose intimate dependence upon her seems to make them a part of her own person and individuality.

Something of these subtle laws of heredity was known even to the ancients, but the greatest acquisitions of knowledge along these lines have come to mankind during the past two centuries. Thomas Andrew Knight, who was born at Wormley Grange, England, in 1758, and died in 1836, accomplished such large results with vegetables, fruits and domestic animals, that he has quite properly been considered the founder of the science of horticulture. It was he who put into practice the principles which have resulted in giving us the improved apples, pears and many other fruits which have been developed from the unpalatable wild varieties. The effects later accomplished by Bakewell in the marvelous improvements in the new Leicester sheep afford one of many striking illustrations. It is said that in the results effected by scientific breeders "it would seem as if they had at first drawn a perfect form and then given it life." Having first determined what form of sheep they preferred, they continued to select from the flocks those which most nearly approached the model, until they attained results which in their standard of perfection were greatly removed from the original type.

If you compare the wild boar of the forests with the improved breeds of swine, the results which have been secured become very manifest. An excellent judge of pigs says: "Pigs' legs should be no longer than just to prevent the animal's belly from trailing on the ground. The leg is the least profitable portion of the hog, and we therefore require no more of it than is absolutely necessary for the support of the rest. Let any one compare the wild boar with any improved breed and he will see how effectually the legs have been shortened."

Breeders of birds and pigeons and poultry have accomplished in their departments similar results. It is to the results of such study and development that we owe the many varieties of poultry, pigeons and birds. The poultry raiser may now determine whether he desires birds with large bodies for the table, or the smaller egg-producers, or whether he prefers other qualities, and he may select from the different varieties such as are possessed of the desired requisites.

When we remember what has been accomplished by those who have taken the single-leaf wild rose and produced the many elaborate and beautiful varieties of roses which are now cultivated in hot-houses, and when we see what has been accomplished by taking the many wild flowers of the field and developing them into the beauty and splendor of what is to be found in the botanical gardens, one gets a very fair idea of what has really been accomplished in these directions. In writing of this subject Dr. M. L. Holbrook says: " If there was no law of heredity, if animals and plants did not transmit their characters to their offspring, then it would be a waste of time to try to improve either." But the horticulturists take advantage of these known laws for the improvement of the original plant, and it is to the application of these same principles that we owe the changes which have transformed the size and flavor of the wild cherry and the wild grape into our present luscious specimens of cultivated fruit.

In the raising, mating and development of birds, sheep and cattle, wonderful results may be secured when the various steps are guarded and directed by intelligence. While it is true that in the mating of human beings all is largely left to sentiment, chance and blind blundering, and while wonderful results could be attained could intelligence and forethought give direction in human love affairs, yet with human beings who intelligently set themselves to correct mistakes and to develop talents, to supply deficiencies and prepare to transmit the very best results that are possible to them, the effort is approved by results in the offspring which are most gratifying and satisfactory.

No one can doubt the law of hereditary transmission. Our inherited and acquired characteristics are sure to be transmitted to our descendants. Indeed, so thoroughly does character permeate one's entire being that it might be said of each drop of blood that in its characteristics it is a miniature of the person in whose body it was secreted. Eminent characters do not emanate from degenerate parents; and neither is the reverse true, except as the result of adequate reversionary influences. It is possible for almost any stock to revert to its original type, but even such results are not produced without adequate causes. True, we have the sentence " Degenerate sons of noble sires," but when one does see such a result he may often find adequate causes. Eminent men often have their powers overtaxed by excessive demands. Great lawyers, physicians, preachers and statesmen often have such incessant demands upon their time and energy that, although some are possessed of great powers of endurance, yet many of them are almost always in a state of physical and mental depletion. Personally they have wrought into their daily effort all that they have to transmit, and their children receive only the remnants and dregs of greatness—a depleted body and a depleted mind.

Sometimes the degeneracy to the lower type

is due to indulgence in social or other vices. If the father is guilty of sexual excesses, given to the liberal use of tobacco, or uses intoxicating liquors, it will not be necessary to look further for the causes. Sometimes the child has had a great father, but a very ordinary mother; or both parents may have been great, while the mother may have been placed under the most disadvantageous surroundings, and subjected to the most unfavorable conditions during the period of gestation; or, after the birth of the child, it may have been turned over to the degenerating influences of diseased and corrupting servants; or it might be that the child had inherited the real character of a father whose reputation was great, but whose character was ordinary. The farmer who would raise a good crop finds three things essential. The first is, good seed; the second is, good soil; and the third is, good care.

CHAPTER XVIII.

PRENATAL INFLUENCES.

SPACE does not permit us to go into a full discussion of the theories and of the principles which lie at the basis of prenatal influences. A few illustrations, however, will be suggestive, induce thoughtful consideration, and possibly lead many to a fuller investigation of the subject.

It is said that the mother of Robert Burns, the Scottish poet, was of a very happy disposition, and evinced a remarkable memory for old songs and ballads, and these she would sing as she went about her daily household duties.

Another instance often named is that of Napoleon Bonaparte. During the months preceding his birth his mother is said to have accompanied her husband on horseback upon one of his military campaigns. For several months she lived in the midst of military surroundings, and became personally interested in the arts of war. These influences stamped their impress upon her unborn child, whose earliest manifestation of childish interest after his birth was an exhibition of the warlike spirit. His thoughts and boyhood conversation were of war and conquest.

Mr. C. J. Bayer, in his interesting and suggestive book, entitled " Maternal Impressions," tells of a woman who, during the period of gestation, was stinted in her allowance of money, and stole from the cash-drawer in her husband's store. The son that was born to them was a kleptomaniac, whose stealing was limited to those of his own family and relatives. He stole his sister's watch, his mother's gold chain, a new suit and a diamond pin from his father; but he was never known to take anything from any one except his near relatives. If mothers would have honest children they should be careful to entertain no dishonest inclinations.

The result of an unsuccessful effort to murder one's own unborn offspring is seen in Guiteau, the assassin who shot President Garfield in 1881. His father was a man of some intellectual ability and integrity of character. The Guiteau children were born in rapid succession, and, because of lack of means, the mother, who was in poor health, was obliged to work harder than would have otherwise been the case. Before the birth of this child she resorted to every means in her power, by the use of drugs, to produce an abortion. In this she was unsuccessful. For several weeks during the latter part of her pregnancy she had brain fever, which probably also had the effect of arresting the development of some parts of the brain of her child. When the child was born it was weak and puny, and for months its life was one continual wail. It was months before the nervous system became at all quiet. He was deficient in common sense, without self-control, and entirely destitute of every vestige of remorse or shame. He was born a degenerate and a murderer.

From the great mass of matter which is available upon the subject of prenatal influences, Dr. Napheys tells of the artist Flaxman, the outlines of whose drawings used to be regarded as the most perfect and graceful in existence: "From earliest childhood he manifested a delight in drawing. His mother, a woman of refinement and artistic taste, used to relate that for months previous to his birth she spent hours daily studying engravings, and fixing in her memory the most beautiful productions of the human figure as portrayed by masters. She was convinced that the genius of her son was the fruit of her own self-culture."

Only a few days ago a young mother who had been alone much of the time during the period of gestation, and who had found special delight in books and reading, called our attention to the fact that her twin girls, now nearly two years of age, will accept a book in preference to toys, and be contented by the hour simply to hold and handle a book.

Mr. C. J. Bayer tells of a young wife at whom some girl friends pointed their finger, and, referring to her condition, said: "Aren't you ashamed of yourself?" After they were gone, the young mother went to her room and cried bitterly over the remark which the girls had made. Her child, when seen by Mr. Bayer at the age of six, if any one, a stranger or friend, pointed a finger at her, would burst into a fit of crying, and it seemed impossible to cure her of this habit.

He also tells of a young mother who had an exceptionally bright child: "When the child was three months old its brightness was commented upon by some of her friends, and the mother said, 'I impressed that upon her.' 'How did you come to do that?' She replied, 'I have seen so many dull children, in my school work, who could not understand what was told them, that I wanted my child to be quick to perceive and to comprehend, and so let my mind dwell upon it, hoping to get favorable results. I had been told that it could be done, and I am convinced that it is possible.'"

Many instances of horrible child-marking are given in medical books, but it is not best to allow the mind to dwell upon these things. We name but a couple of instances, to illustrate the principle. Dr. Napheys tells of a woman, the wife of a baker, who, during the early months of her pregnancy, sold bread over the counter. Nearly every day a child with a double thumb came in for a penny roll, presenting the money between the thumb and the finger. After the third month the mother left the bakery, but the malformation was so impressed upon her mind that she was not surprised to see it reproduced in her own infant. The mother in due time sought to correct the deformity by having the supernumerary thumb removed by a surgical operation.

We recently heard of a mother who gave birth to a child that had but one hand. The other arm was handless, as if amputated between the elbow and wrist. The only way she could account for the deficiency in her child was the fact that her husband's brother, who had had his hand amputated, lived in the family during the earlier months of her pregnancy. While she received no special shock, being familiar with his condition, yet the mental impression, continued through a considerable period of the earlier months, had its disastrous result.

Mr. C. J. Bayer names some interesting instances in support of his theory that the disastrous effects of being frightened in the earlier months of gestation may be corrected by the wish of the mother that her child may not be affected, deformed or marked by the object or influences which have caused her to be startled. He says that if a mother earnestly desires to counteract a bad influence she should hope and long that it may not do any harm. The result of such mental effort will be beneficial to the forming brain. That very longing and desire upon the part of the mother will have a corresponding effect upon her child. This idea is drawn from, and the phenomena is explained by, the fact that the mother, through her longings, creates the brain-substance which is to control the desires which her child will possess.

Much might also be said upon the subject of

longings. In a general way it may be said that it is always best, when the longing is a proper one, to see that it is promptly gratified. Even a desire for a particular article of food is likely to produce in the child a pronounced desire for the same thing. It is well, also, for the mother carefully to note any longings which occur during the period of gestation, as it may afford her an easy clue to the cause of the persistent crying of her child after its birth. An instance may prove suggestive.

An Israelitish mother, "before the birth of her first child, smelled fried pork, and longed for a taste of it, but her religion forbade. When the child was born he positively refused the breast or bottle. The nurse asked: 'What does this child want?' The mother replied: 'I do not know of anything, except pork.' The father at once got a strip of pork, let the child suck it a few moments, after which he was ready to nurse." The father also related that notwithstanding the fact that the eating of pork was contrary to their religious teaching, yet they had never been able to restrain their son, who was then twenty-one years of age, from eating it.

Numerous instances are related in different books where young infants have moaned and cried continually, and upon being given a taste of that for which the mother had longed prior to the birth of the child the infant at once became quiet, and afterward seemed passive and contented.

We have read of a young mother who was

a strict temperance woman, but who had a longing for liquor. Her husband was also a temperance man, but they decided that some be given the mother, the same as any other medicine, under the circumstances, in order to relieve the longing and save the child. After taking a dose of liquor the longing passed away, and the child was normally born. Where the use of liquor is persisted in during the period of pregnancy, many instances might be quoted where all the children in the family died drunkards. There are some exceptional instances in which the children of intemperate fathers never seem possessed of a desire to use beverages. It is possible that investigation might show, in such instances, that the mother had such an abhorrence of the effects of intemperance upon her huband that her constant longing that her children might live sober, upright lives had resulted in securing for her a strictly temperance progeny.

Dr. Dio Lewis, in his book entitled "Chastity," when writing of prenatal influences, says: "It is not carrying this subject too far to say that if any trade or profession seems particularly desirable, the genius for success in that line may be given to the child by proper effort before its birth. The mother whose mind persistently dwells upon any chosen subject during this nine months of gestation will surely see in her offspring the mark of her thought. Beauty of person, strength of mind, sweetness of disposition and holy aspiration may be assured to posterity by parents wise and loving enough to fulfill the laws which lead to the desired results."

Dr. Napheys, in writing upon the same subject, says: "What a charming idea is this! What an incentive, to those about to become mothers, to cultivate refinement, high thoughts, pure emotion, elevated sentiments!"

The character and disposition of the children oftentimes indicate the influences which surrounded the mother during the months prior to their birth. The first-born is likely to resemble the father more closely than the children born later, because the bride is apt to have her thoughts dwell much upon her young husband. Those born during a period of financial prosperity are likely to be liberal, sometimes wasteful, and, possibly, spendthrifts. Those born during the years when means are scarce and economy is necessary are likely to be economical, and some even miserly.

Prenatal influences are both subtle and potent, and no amount of wealth or learning or influence can secure exemption from them. No golden lock or jeweled hand can successfully hold the door against the admission of these influences. Medical science has done much to mend defects, alleviate suffering, patch up broken constitutions, and effect great improvements, but the greatest remains to be accomplished by remedying, as far as possible, the causes of these great evils by disseminating intelligence and inspiring parents and young people with such knowledge and purposes as will prepare the way for the raising up of a superior generation. In this work the philanthropic physician occupies the place of greatest usefulness.

Parents need to realize that the work of right-forming is greater than the work of reforming. The philanthropist who labors for the reformation of adults does well; those who give their energy and effort to the education and proper bringing up of children do better; but those who intelligently devote themselves to the proper formation of the body, character and disposition of those yet unborn do best of all. We are thoroughly orthodox upon the subject of human depravity, but we believe that persons may be so generated as to be the more easy subjects of regeneration. Or they may be so " conceived and born in sin " as manifestly to illustrate the declaration of the Psalmist: "The wicked are estranged from the womb; they go astray as soon as they are born."

Before leaving this subject we desire to say a word which may be of comfort to any parents whose children may be born to them with some blemish or deformity. God has so equipped the mother-heart and the father-heart that they should love and care for those who are unattractive, or even unsightly. We recently heard of a mother whose child was born with a harelip, and, fearing lest the sight of the child might have a depressing effect upon the mother in her enfeebled condition, various excuses were made to keep the child out of her sight for a period of several days. When evasions would avail no longer, and the mother was shown her child, after a momentary sense of disappointment she said: "Well, it is my child, and I can love it just the same.'

It is also an encouragement to know that what are ordinarily called birthmarks generally diminish, and oftentimes disappear after a brief period. Dr. Russegger tells of a woman who in the seventh month of her pregnancy was bitten in the calf of her leg by a dog. At the moment of the accident she was somewhat alarmed, but neither then nor afterward had any fear that her child would be affected by the occurrence. Ten weeks later, when her child was born, there were marks upon the calf of its right leg resembling the impressions made by the dog's teeth upon the leg of the mother. The impressions of two of the teeth disappeared in five weeks, and the others gradually faded away. Similar results may be expected in most instances.

There is one branch of the prenatal subject which has reference to determining the sex before birth, in which some persons, because of a predominance of either male or female children in their families, may naturally and properly have special interest. The desire of some parents for male children in preference to female children is both wrong and unworthy of that proper Christian regard in which woman should rightfully be held. In heathen countries, because of the hardships to which women are subjected, the parents are often sad when a girl is born into the family; but in Christian lands, where the influences of the gospel have given woman her proper place and rightful recognition, the feeling which disparages the girl child, or would lead to a preference for male children to the exclusion of female children, is altogether wrong and unworthy of our Christian civilization.

It will readily be seen, from the effect of prenatal influences, that it would not be desirable, because of its effects upon the formation of the growing life within the mother's body, that she should allow her mind to dwell largely upon these subjects, or anxiously desire one sex in preference to another. Where such influences are exerted upon the embryo, a male child with an effeminate, girlish nature, or a female child with a boyish, masculine disposition, might be the result. While it is perfectly proper that parents should know what views are held by medical and scientific men upon these subjects, it is not best that the mother's mind should be influenced by the consideration of them during the period of gestation.

The influences which control and determine sex are so subtle, and have hitherto so thoroughly evaded human investigation and study, that little or no reliance can be placed upon any of the theories. Of the vast number of theories, many are ludicrous, some are exact contraries of others, a few seem plausible, while none have been found infallible, or even reliable.

Some have held that the phases of the moon at the period of conception controlled and determined the sex of the offspring. Others have held that the season of the year when the ovum is produced and fertilized determines the result. This theory makes it largely a question of temperature and climate. The theory which has had many advocates is one that contends that the question of sex is largely determined by the question of food prior to conception and during the period of gestation. By persons who hold this theory it is maintained that during periods of prosperity and plenty the number of girl children preponderate, and that during periods of adversity, and when food is less abundant, the majority of those who are born are boys. Another theory which has been often repeated, and as often disproved, is that the sex of the offspring is determined by the side of the reproductive system engaged in the production of the ovum, and of the sperm; that if the generative glands upon the right side of the body of the mother and of the father are engaged, a male child is the result; but if the left sides are engaged, the result is a girl. This theory maintains that the ovum which proceeds from the right ovary results in the formation of the body of a male child, while those that proceed from the left ovary result in the production of a female child. That this theory is not reliable has often been demonstrated in instances where the right or the left ovary of the woman has been removed by surgical operation, and she has subsequently become the mother both of male and of female offspring. The same is true with regard to fathers who have, by accident or disease, lost one of the testes, and have subsequently become the fathers of both boys and girls.

Another theory which has received considerable attention is that the ova, liberated from month to month, alternate in gender. That one month the ovum is of that character which would result in the production of a male child, and the succeeding month of such a nature as would result in the production of a female child. Some hold that the respective ages of the parents have something to do with determining the question of the sex of their offspring; that where the father is older than the mother, female children are likely to predominate. Some hold that the superior vitality of the father, or of the mother, will result in the production of sex of their own kind. Some persons who have given attention and study to this subject teach exactly the reverse of these two theories.

The theory which has been largely accepted by intelligent medical authorities is that children conceived in from two to six days after the cessation of the menses are generally girls, and that those conceived in from nine to twelve days after the cessation of the menses are boys—or, in other words, that those begotten in the earlier period after the cessation of the monthly period of the mother are likely to be girls, and those begotten in the latter period are likely to be boys.

There are many theories, some of which seem altogether fanciful, if not silly—such as that the sex of the child is determined by the side of the bed upon which the father sleeps, whether the bed is situated so that the persons lie with their heads toward the north or some other point of the compass. Knowing the natural curiosity of not a few persons upon such subjects, and the abnormal desire of some parents for children of one or the other sex, there are not a few impostors who offer to furnish information upon these subjects at a costly price. The methods proposed are sometimes innocent, and may be without injury, while in many other instances the suggestions are debasing, likely to produce injurious results, and never reliable. While the desired sex may be determined in harmony with natural laws, the parents may give all the credit to the impostor, if Nature has brought them a child of the sex they have desired. It would scarcely seem necessary to advise intelligent people against the impositions of such ignorant pretenders.

The entire subject has been wrapped in a mystery hitherto impenetrable. No investigation has yet been able to secure from Nature her secret concerning this matter. It is very possible that the Creator of mankind has purposely placed this knowledge beyond human reach, and left the regulation of this important matter wholly to His own infinite decrees.

CHAPTER XIX.

CHILDHOOD.

WHILE it is possibly true that the most potent molding influences may be exerted prior to the birth of the child, yet where parents have lacked the intelligence to avail themselves of the largest and best results in this respect, or discover defects after their children are born, there still remains an opportunity for them. They can in some measure retrieve lost opportunities, correct defects, supply deficiencies, and even accomplish wonderful results in the training and development of their children. "As the twig is bent the tree is inclined." If the twig is crooked, if taken very early it may be straightened; but it is far better that the twig should be straight at first, and without the necessity of being straightened. It is better that children should be born without defects, rather than that there should be the necessity of correcting these mistakes; but as a straight twig may be bent to its permanent and incurable injury, so a child, properly nurtured and well-born, may be injured or totally ruined, mentally, morally or physically, by deficient or defective training during its childhood.

There are many excellent books upon the nurture and training of children, and young parents would do well to avail themselves of the advantages and excellent suggestions afforded by such publications. There are also many excellent periodicals for young parents, such as "The New Crusade," "Trained Motherhood," "The Mothers' Journal," and others, which are very valuable and almost indispensable. From such books and periodicals young parents can obtain the best of suggestions with regard to the early care, proper nurture and careful training of their little ones. We cannot now dwell upon any of the many important phases of child-training. Space only affords opportunity to emphasize some things which seem to us of special importance and likely to be overlooked.

Many young parents think that the training of their children will be a matter for consideration when they are three or four years old. No more serious mistake can possibly be made. The first three months will determine the babyhood, and the first two years the childhood, and the childhood will determine the manhood or womanhood. The first two years may almost be said to determine both the character and the destiny of the child for all time to come. The child that is not properly taught during the first two years is likely to remain untaught, undisciplined, uncontrolled, and oftentimes uncontrollable, for the remainder of its childhood and throughout its entire life.

The questions of the hours of feeding, the hours for sleep; whether the child is to be rocked, or carried when it whimpers—all these are questions of the utmost importance from the very beginning. Many a mother has been enslaved for life because of the mistakes which she made during the first few weeks after her child was born.

Parents should protect their children against the silly and dangerous habit of being promiscuously kissed. The prevalent custom of kissing babies and children is not only silly upon the part of those who do it, but a nuisance to the child, and in many instances detrimental to the health of the child. Where promiscuous kissing is allowed, persons with offensive breath, consumptive tendencies, contagious and even loathsome diseases, may unintentionally inflict irreparable wrong upon both the child and its parents. Only the other day we read in a medical journal where a young child of poor parents who kept a boarding-house was kissed by one of the boarders, who communicated to the child one of the most loathsome of diseases. Such dangers exist not only among the poor, but are perhaps even more prevalent among the affluent, in the circle of whose acquaintances there is likely to be some well-dressed but vicious and corrupt individual.

Let no care or proper expense be spared in making the influences which are exerted in the nursery both attractive and potent. Young parents should be their children's best playfellows. There should be a proper amount of games, carefully-selected amusements, books, papers, pictures chosen with scrupulous care, and mother and mother's influence in the midst of them all. What the child needs pre-eminently above playthings, books, clothes, and every other earthly thing, is *the presence and influence of mother*. No other woman in the world can take her place. Many mothers farm their children out to nurses, and then give themselves to household duties, social pleasures, or possibly to duties which may be important in themselves, but which, after all, can only be secondary to the discharge of the all-important duties of motherhood.

Many otherwise excellent women find the nursery a prison, and the care of their own children irksome, simply because they have a perverted mother-sense. The mother should have proper relief from the care of her children, but if she has the true mother-heart the companionship of her children will be the society which she will prefer above that of all others.

Where servants are necessary, and such cases do exist, parents should exercise the utmost caution in guarding the purity of their children. Hundreds, and we can properly say thousands, of children are annually wronged and ruined by the vices practiced upon them by servants. This is an especial danger where nurses and servants are permitted to undress the child and put it to bed at night. Many a nurse who is anxious to quiet her little charge, that it may fall asleep promptly, is guilty of exciting sensations which quiet the child and prevent its crying, but which inflict upon the nervous system of an infant results of the most far-reaching character. Mothers are very apt to be unsuspecting in these matters, and therefore it is highly important that the attention of fathers should be called to this grave danger.

The child should also be protected against being frightened, being made afraid in the dark, told of spooks, bugaboos, "the old beggar-man" and the police coming for them. Remember, also, that in this most impressible period of character-formation servants and others can do the child great injury by teaching it to be deceitful and untruthful. It is at this age, also, that they learn incorrect and ungrammatical forms of expression; and if the nurse-girl is ignorant and silly, and is permitted to assemble upon the streets or in the park, with others of her age, while tending the child, a bright child of two or three years will pick up more coarseness and more undesirable information concerning human depravity than can be expunged from its mind by subsequent months and years of careful training.

It is important to enjoin upon parents the duty of guarding their children against secret vice. Parents are very apt to think that while other children might be guilty of such sins, their own children are "too innocent and too pure" to fall into such vices. We have known mothers to hold up their hands in holy horror at such a suggestion, but when the more cautious fathers have watched their children, they have discovered that even at the age of five and six their little boys have learned from older playmates, impure companions, degraded servants, or by sliding down the balustrade, or in some other incidental way, the terrible habit of self-pollution. Young children cannot be too carefully guarded in this important matter. Where infants exhibit a tendency to handle their private parts, great care should be given to the cleanliness of those parts, and, if continued, the family physician should be consulted, to see whether circumcision is not necessary to remove local irritation and inflammation. This is found to be necessary in many instances. Circumcision was an important sanitary regulation among the Israelites, is a simple surgical operation which is most beneficial in its results, and very important in many instances.

When your children are old enough to ask honest questions, see that, in reply, they receive an honest answer. If a child is intelligent and thoughtful, one of the earliest inquiries will be concerning the origin of life. When a little one is born into your own or another household, it is only natural and proper that intelligent children should inquire where it came from. There should be no fables about babies being brought by doctors, or being found under cabbage-leaves, or taken from hollow stumps in the woods, for an intelligent and altogether satisfactory answer can be given to an intelligent child of six or seven years, and even younger. Another has aptly and truthfully said: "Ignorance is a deadly sin. The truth properly told has never yet harmed a child; silence, false modesty and mystery have corrupted the souls and bodies of untold millions." Where parents are intelligent upon this subject, and know how to present these matters properly to the thought of their children, we have never heard of a child who asked an embarrassing question, nor have we known of anything but the most satisfactory and blessed results. Parents will find beautiful and helpful suggestions in " Teaching Truth " and " Child Confidence Rewarded," two booklets by Mary Wood-Allen, M.D.; and it was also to aid parents in these matters that " What a Young Boy Ought to Know " and " What a Young Girl Ought to Know " were written. Parents should read these books and learn how to communicate the information, either in conversation or by reading to the child such portions as are suited to its needs. Remember that the disposition which prompts your child to keep an unclean thing a secret from you will also incline the child to refrain from conversation upon a pure matter which is to be a secret between parent and child. If you allow others to teach your child sacred truths in an unhallowed way, if you decline to give your children an honest answer to their honest and reasonable inquiries, they will secure in its degrading form, from vicious companions or ignorant servants, the information they seek. It is infinitely easier to keep the mind of the child pure than to purify it after it has been polluted. When corrupting thoughts and degrading pictures have been painted upon the canvas of the mind, they can never be totally obliterated.

When your child approaches the age of puberty, the little boy becomes awkward, his voice breaks, the down starts upon his upper lip, he becomes bashful and shrinking. At that trying period, when so many take special pleasure in taunting and tantalizing—at that period of special stress when the boy and the girl preeminently need tenderness—see to it that your children are protected against the wrongs to which others are subjected. This is the period in the life of the boy and the girl when they are not able to understand themselves or to interpret life to their own satisfaction, and then it is that they should be made intelligent upon the conditions which attend the transition from childhood, and indicate the approach of manhood and womanhood. It is then that the books in the series for boys and girls will be found especially indispensable, and in due time, according to the judgment of the parents, should be followed by the book addressed to young men or to young women.

Look carefully after the education of your children. Remember that the picture-book, the nursery-song, the evening prayer, the family music, the walk, the ride, the hasty word, the thoughtful counsel, are all helping to educate your child. Know what books they read. Be sure that in the public schools they sit under the instruction of no one who insinuates doubt or destroys the careful and sacred instruction of the home. When evening comes and evil lurks for the destruction of the young, gather your children about you in your home. Make home attractive to them. Let it be the centre and source of that which is to inspire them to noble manhood and exalted womanhood. Regard nothing as expensive which will contribute to make your children pure and good and great.

That your children may be guarded against the errors which come from sleeping with other children, neither at home nor elsewhere should they share their beds with others.

Look well to the physical culture of your children. If physical culture has no place in your school, see that the attention of directors and teachers is called to this important matter. Encourage your children to use the gymnasium of the Young Men's Christian Association, or some other organization that similarly maintains the strictest purity and the highest moral standards. Teach or have your children taught those forms of gymnastics that require no appurtenances; supply them with a pair of dumb-bells weighing a pound or two each. Furnish the nursery with some Exerciser of approved pattern, with preference for one which can be adjusted to the needs of either adults or children. Encourage them in out-of-door sports; see that their sleeping-rooms are well ventilated; encourage them to desire to be strong and well. Teach them to govern their appetites; regulate their lives so as to secure the best health and the best physical and intellectual powers.

In the culture of the intellectual and the physical do not forget the moral training of your children. Among the books and the papers, see that there is a good supply of those of a religious character. Teach your children to want right things, and to have pleasure in doing good. Make a faithful use of the Sunday-school and of the Church. Let their place in the family pew from early childhood be regularly filled; provide them with a hymn-book, see that they have something for the collection, teach them to be reverent. If, in early life, your children are religiously inclined, do not make the fatal mistake of standing between them and their union with the Church. Do not say: "Oh! they are too young fully to understand what it all means." Who is old enough to understand all the mysteries of Divine grace? It is enough for us to know that Jesus welcomes and saves the children, as well as older people. Polycarp was converted at nine years of age; Matthew Henry at eleven; President Edwards at seven; Dr. Watts at nine; Bishop Hall at seven, and Robert Hall at twelve.

And now we have come to the place where author and reader must part. Taking your hand in a final grasp, we can only look into your face and assure you that if, as a young husband, you rightly estimate the sacredness of marriage; if you bring to it that purity, honor and sanctity which you rightly expect upon the part of your wife; if you rightly use its privileges, and are ready to exercise such personal restraints as shall secure to both parties the largest present pleasure and permanent happiness, you will then obtain the benediction and blessings which marriage and home and parentage have to bestow.

THE END.

OFFICES OF PUBLICATION

IN THE UNITED STATES
THE VIR PUBLISHING COMPANY
2237 LAND TITLE BUILDING
PHILADELHHIA, PA.

IN ENGLAND
THE VIR PUBLISHING COMPANY
7 IMPERIAL ARCADE, LUDGATE CIRCUS
LONDON, E. C.

IN CANADA
WILLIAM BRIGGS
29-33 RICHMOND STREET WEST
TORONTO, ONTARIO

"What a Young Boy Ought to Know."
BY SYLVANUS STALL, D. D.
Condensed Table of Contents

PART I.

God's purpose in endowing plants, animals and man with reproductive power—The question of the origin of life a natural and proper one—Difference between creating and making—How God now creates or reproduces the flowers, insects, fishes and animals—The mamma and papa plants and the baby plants—The mamma and papa nature in the stalk of corn—The two natures united in the same flower—Separated in other plants—The office of the wind and insects in fertilizing the flowers—The mamma and papa natures united in the same oyster—The life of the baby oyster—The two natures separated in the fishes—The eggs and the baby fishes—How seeds are made to grow and how eggs are hatched—The beautiful lives of parent birds—The bird's nest, the eggs and the baby birds—Why the eggs of animals may not be exposed in a nest—The nest which God has prepared for them—The hatching of the egg or the birth of the animal—The creation of Adam and Eve—God created man with power similar to his creative power—The purity of parentage.

PART II

The manner in which the reproductive organs are injured in boys by abuse—Comparative anatomy, or points of resemblance between bodies of birds, animals and man—Man the only animal with a perfect hand—With the hand he constructs, builds and blesses—With the hand he smites, slays and injures others, and degrades himself.

PART III

The consequences in boys of the abuse of the reproductive organs—Need of proper information—The moral effects first to manifest themselves—How secret sin affects the character of boys—Effects upon the body and the nerves—Effects upon the brain and mind—The physical effects that follow.

PARTS IV and V

How boys may preserve their bodies in purity and strength—Our duty to aid others to avoid pernicious habits, and to retain or regain their purity and strength.

PARTS VI and VII

How purity and strength may be measurably regained—The age of adolescence or puberty and its attendant changes—Its significance and its dangers.

Price, {$1.00 / 4 s.} net, post free

"What a Young Boy Ought to Know"

For Boys under Sixteen Years of Age

WHAT EMINENT PEOPLE SAY

Theodore L. Cuyler, D.D.
"'What a Young Boy Ought to Know' ought to be in every home where there is a boy."

Lady Henry Somerset
"Calculated to do an immense amount of good. I sincerely hope it may find its way to many homes."

Joseph Cook, D.D., LL.D.
"It is everywhere suggestive, inspiring and strategic in a degree, as I think, not hitherto matched in literature of its class."

Charles L. Thompson, D.D.
"Why was not this book written centuries ago?"

Anthony Comstock
"It lifts the mind and thoughts upon a high and lofty plane upon delicate subjects."

Edward W. Bok
"It has appealed to me in a way which no other book of its kind has."

Bishop John H. Vincent, D.D., LL.D.
"You have handled with great delicacy and wisdom an exceedingly difficult subject."

John Willis Baer
"I feel confident that it can do great good, and I mean that my boys shall have the contents placed before them."

Mrs. Mary A. Livermore, LL.D.
"Full of physiological truths, which all children ought to know, at a proper age; will be read by boys without awakening a prurient thought."

Josiah Strong, D.D.
"A foolish and culpable silence on the part of most parents leaves their children to learn, too often from vicious companions, sacred truth in an unhallowed way."

"What a Young Man Ought to Know."

BY SYLVANUS STALL, D. D.

Condensed Table of Contents

STRENGTH

The value of physical strength—the weak man handicapped—Three-fold nature of man—Relation of the physical, intellectual and moral—Impair one, you injure all—The physical foundation—Man's strong sexual nature—Sexuality strongly marked in all great men—Importance of manly mastery of sexual nature—Personal purity—Only one moral standard for men and women.

WEAKNESS

Inherited weakness—How overcome—Acquired weakness—How produced—The effects of secret vice—What should be done—Losses in sleep—When to consult a physician—Danger from quacks and charlatans—What are normal and abnormal losses—Medical authorities quoted—Subject illustrated—Important directions.

SOCIAL VICE

Alarming ignorance concerning the diseases which accompany vice—Why physicians do not acquaint their patients with the nature of these diseases—The prevalence—All forms of venereal diseases leave terrible results—Character and consequences of gonorrhœa—Later complications—Chordee, stricture, blindness, etc.—How healthy brides become early and permanent invalids—Chancroid and chancre—The primary, secondary and tertiary forms of syphilis—The beginning, progress and end—Can it ever be cured—May the man ever marry—Effects upon wife and children.

THE REPRODUCTIVE ORGANS

Their purpose and prostitution—Marriage a great blessing—Difference between creation and procreation—All life from the seed or the egg—The reproduction of plants, fishes, birds and animals contrasted—An interesting study

MAN'S RELATION TO WOMAN

Importance of a right relation to women—The nature of marriage—The friends and foes of marriage—Who should not marry—The selection of a wife—Some general rules—Importance of great caution—Causes of unhappiness in married life—Early and late marriages.

HINDRANCES AND HELPS

The choice of companions, books, pictures, amusements, recreations—Liquors and tobacco—Self-mastery—Right aim in life—Industry, early rising—The influence of an ennobling affection—Education—The Sabbath, the Church and the Bible.

Price $\left\{ \begin{array}{l} \$1.00 \\ 4\text{ s.} \end{array} \right\}$ net, per copy, post free

"What a Young Man Ought to Know"

WHAT EMINENT PEOPLE SAY

Francis E. Clark, D. D.

"It is written reverently but very plainly, and I believe will save a multitude of young men from evils unspeakable."

John Clifford, D. D.

"One of the best books for dawning manhood that has fallen into my hands. It goes to the roots of human living. It is thoroughly manly."

J. Wilbur Chapman, D. D.

"I bear willing testimony that I believe this book ought to be in the hands of every young man in this country."

Paul F. Munde, M. D., LL. D.

Professor of Gynæcology in the New York Polyclinic and at Dartmouth College.

"I most heartily commend not only the principle but the execution of what it aims to teach."

The Right Rev. William N. McVickar, D. D.

"I heartily endorse and recommend 'What a Young Man Ought to Know.' I believe that it strikes at the very root of matters."

Ethelbert D. Warfield, LL. D.

"The subject is one of the utmost personal and social importance, and hitherto has not been treated, so far as I am aware, in such a way as to merit the commendation of the Christian public."

Frank W. Ober

"It will save many a young fellow from the blast and blight of a befouled manhood, wrecked by the wretched blunderings of an ignorant youth."

Frederick Anthony Atkins

"Such books as yours have long been needed, and if they had appeared sooner many a social wreck, whose fall was due to ignorance, might have been saved."

"What a Man of Forty-five Ought to Know."
BY SYLVANUS STALL, D. D.
Condensed Table of Contents

PART I
WHAT HE OUGHT TO KNOW CONCERNING HIMSELF

Prevalent ignorance concerning physical changes in men of middle-life—Sad results of such ignorance—Reasons for change—Evidences of these changes—Husband and wife constitute a reproductive unit—The two natures responsive in activity and repose—Somewhat similar changes in both—The age at which climacteric or "change of life" occurs in men—Climacteric and adolescence contrasted—The testimony of medical men to the fact—Only young men need the testimonials of authorities—Old men know it—Compensations which follow the sexual hush—Physical and mental effects—Changes more gradual than in women—Many men intellectually at their best after sexual hush—To them time and experience open their richest treasures—Moderation in all things enjoined—Sexual moderation emphasized—Virility, how destroyed, how preserved—Effects of exercise, food, stimulants, sleep, employment, etc.—Functional disorders—Benefit of intelligence—Enlargement of the prostate gland—Manifestations, cause and precautionary measures—The marriage of men of middle life—Physical unfitness and effects—Rights of the unborn—The years beyond—The man at forty determines what the man at eighty shall be—Value of purpose to keep strong and bright—Examples.

PART II
WHAT HE OUGHT TO KNOW CONCERNING HIS WIFE

Reproduction the primal purpose of marriage—Attractive and repellent periods in life of woman—Climacteric or change of life the most repellent period—Disappearance of menstruation only an outward manifestation—The phenomenon explained—Reasons for change made plain—Not a period of stress for all women—How to meet the menopause—Occupation, diet, fresh air, exercise, sleep, companionship, sexual repose, etc., etc.—Mortality and insanity greater among men—The aches and ills which attend the menopause—Aversion to husband, children and friends—Physical changes which attend and follow change of life in women—Modified sexual nature—Growths—Mental changes and conditions—Need of intelligence upon the part of husband and others.

Price { $1.00 / 4 s. } net, post free

"What a Man of Forty-five Ought to Know"

PRAISED BY THE PRESS

"We do not hesitate to recommend."—*Experience.*

"A reliable and instructive guide in se---- matters and yet pure and chaste in style."—*Jo--nal of Dermatology.*

"Information of vital importance —*Pittsburgh Christian Advocate.*

"Written in an honest, frank and fearless way."—*Christian Standard.*

"It is a clean book which one should sit down to alone."—*The Evangelist.*

"These books deserve to be circulated by the million."—*Leslie's Weekly.*

"To many men the guidance of this book will be a timely benediction."—*Chicago Appeal.*

"The utterance of one who has an accurate knowledge of men."—*Brooklyn Citizen.*

"It is a helpful book and in all important particulars sound in its medical statements."—*Baltimore Sun.*

"This book is recommendable not only to the intelligent layman to read himself and hand to others, but also to the physician, who ought to welcome it as a means to refresh an important part of his physiologic knowledge."—*Alkaloidal Clinic.*

"A man who is a fool at forty-five (and there are many of them) is pretty hard to manage. There are certain things which he ought to know without being told, but it is difficult to teach him these things. He needs reasoning with and plain talking to. This book does it in a healthy, elevating manner. These cases are often very troublesome to the physician. It would be well to have this book handy to lend to such patients. This course will help the physician to manage his patient and help the patient. This book will do much good. There has been a need for just such a work."—*Medical World.*

"What a Young Girl Ought to Know."

BY MRS. MARY WOOD-ALLEN, M. D.

Condensed Table of Contents

PART I

The origin of life—One plan in all forms of life—How plants grow from the seed—They feed on the soil, grow and mature.—How the plant reproduces itself—The flower, the pol. 1, the pod, the seed—The office of bees and insects in fei. 'ization.

PART II

Fishes and their young—The parent fishes and the baby fishes—The seeds of plants and eggs of fishes, birds and animals—How fishes never know their baby offspring—Warm blooded animals—Lessons from birds —Their nests, eggs and little ones.

PART III

Animals and their young—The place which God has prepared for their young—Beginning their independent life—Human babies the most helpless and dependent of all creatures—The relations of parent and child—The child a part of each parent—Heredity and its lessons.

PART IV

The value of good health—The care of the body—The body a temple to be kept holy—Girls should receive their instruction from their mothers—The body the garment which the soul wears—Effects of thoughts upon life and character—Value of good companions, good books and good influences—What it is to become a woman.

Price { $1.00 / 4 s. } net, per copy

"What a Young Girl Ought to Know"

WHAT EMINENT PEOPLE SAY

Francis E. Willard, LL. D.

"I do earnestly hope that this book, founded on a strictly scientific but not forgetting a strong ethical basis, may be well known and widely read by the dear girls in their teens and the young women in their homes."

Mrs. Elizabeth B. Grannis

"These facts ought to be judiciously brought to the intelligence of every child whenever it asks questions concerning its own origin."

Mrs. Harriet Lincoln Coolidge

"It is a book that mothers and daughters ought to own."

Mrs. Katharine L. Stevenson

"The book is strong, direct, pure, as healthy as a breeze from the mountain-top."

Mrs. Isabelle MacDonald Alden, "Pansy"

"It is just the book needed to teach what most people do not know how to teach, being scientific, simple and plain-spoken, yet delicate."

Miss Grace H. Dodge

"I know of no one who writes or speaks on these great subjects with more womanly touch than Mrs. Wood-Allen, nor with deeper reverence. When I listen to her I feel that she has been inspired by a Higher Power."

Ira D. Sankey

"Every mother in the land that has a daughter should secure for her a copy of "What a Young Girl Ought to Know." It will save the world untold sorrow"

"What a Young Woman Ought to Know."

BY MRS. MARY WOOD-ALLEN, M. D.

Condensed Table of Contents

PART I

CHILDHOOD AND GROWTH

Woman's worth—Importance of care of the body—How to obtain health—Waste and repair—Questions of food—Importance of rest in sleep—The office and importance of correct breathing—Injuries from tight clothing—Physical culture—Exercise and recreation—The value of the bath.

PART II

WOMANHOOD

The endowment of new powers—The conferring of life—Brain building and character formation—Soul and self—Special physiology—Woman's special bodily endowments—The crisis in the girl's life—Ovulation and menstruation—Their significance—Causes and cures of disturbed physical conditions—Painful periods and displacements—Special care of health at special times—Many healthful suggestions suited to the physical needs of young women—Secret vice and its consequences—The relation of pure young women to young men—Friendships.

PART III

What is love—Should include mental conjugality, spiritual sympathy and physical attraction—Responsibility in marriage—Antecedents, talents and habits of young man—The law of heredity—Beneficial—Effects of stimulants upon offspring—Inherited effects of immorality—Good characteristics also transmitted—Requisites in a husband—Engagements—Benefits of, evils of—Holding to the highest ideals—Weddings—Gifts, tours and realities of life.

Price { $1.00 / 4 s. } net, per copy, post free

"What a Young Woman Ought to Know"

WHAT EMINENT PEOPLE SAY

Lady Henry Somerset

"An extremely valuable book, and I wish that it may be widely circulated."

Mrs. Laura Ormiston Chant

"The book ought to be in the hands of every girl on her fifteenth birthday, as a safe guide and teacher along the difficult path of womanhood."

Margaret Warner Morley

"There is an awful need for the book, and it does what it has undertaken to do better than anything of the kind I ever read."

Mrs. May Wright Sewall

"I am profoundly grateful that a subject of such information to young woman should be treated in a manner at once so noble and so delicate."

Elizabeth Cady Stanton

"It is a grave mistake for parents to try to keep their children ignorant of the very questions on which they should have scientific information."

Lillian M. N. Stevens

"There is a great need of carefully, delicately written books upon the subjects treated in this series. I am gratefully glad that the author has succeeded so well, and I trust great and enduring good will be the result."

Mrs. Matilda B. Carse

"It is pure and instructive on the delicate subjects that mean so much to our daughters, to their future as homekeepers, wives and mothers, and to the future generations."

"What a Young Wife Ought to Know."

BY MRS. EMMA F. A. DRAKE, M. D.

Condensed Table of Contents

HUSBAND AND HOME

The choice of a husband—One worthy of both love and respect—Real characteristics necessary—Purity vs. "wild oats"—What shall a young wife expect to be to her husband?—His equal, but not his counterpart—His helpmeet Wifehood and motherhood—Should keep pace with his mental growth—Trousseau and wedding presents—The foolish and ruinous display at weddings—Wedding presents and unhappiness—Wise choice of furniture—The best adornments for the home.

THE MARITAL RELATIONS

The marital state should be the most holy of sanctuaries—Its influence upon character—Modesty—Reproduction the primal purpose—Love's highest plane—The right and wrong of marriage—The wrongdoings of good men.

PARENTHOOD

Preparation for motherhood—Motherhood the glory of womanhood—Maternity productive of health—Clothing—Exercise—Baths, etc., etc.—The child the expression of the mother's thoughts—The five stages of prenatal culture.

PREPARATION FOR FATHERHOOD

Questions which test the fitness of young men for marriage—Many young men of startling worth—Effects of bad morals and wayward habits—Tobacco and Alcoholics—Attaining the best—The father reproduced in his children.

ANTENATAL INFANTICIDE

The moral responsibility of parents in heredity—The mother's investment of moulding power—Parents workers together with God—Ailments during expectant motherhood—Maternity a normal state—Development of the fœtus—Minuteness of the germ of human life—Changes which take place—Life present the moment conception takes place—The sin of tampering with the work of the Infinite.

THE LITTLE ONE

Baby's wardrobe—The question that comes with fluttering signs of life—Importance of wise choice of material and style of dress—Choice of physician and nurse of real consequence—The birth chamber—Surroundings and after-care of the mother—The care of the baby—The responsibilities and joys of motherhood—The mother the baby's teacher—Common ailments of children and how to treat them—Guarding against vice—The training of children—Body building—Helps for mothers.

Price, { $1.00 / 4 s. } net, post free.

"What a Young Wife Ought to Know"

WHAT EMINENT PEOPLE SAY

Mrs. Margaret E. Sangster

"Joyfully I send you my unqualified endorsement of the excellent book, 'What a Young Wife Ought to Know.' I wish every young and perplexed wife might read its pages."

Mrs. Booker T. Washington

"I spent yesterday and last night reading your book and I wish to say that I consider this book a useful friend to every young woman."

Charles H. Parkhurst, D. D.

"It handles delicate matters in a manner as firm as it is delicate, and dignifies even what is common by the purity of the sentiment and nobility of intent with which it is treated."

Marietta Holly (Josiah Allen's Wife)

"It is an excellent book; if every young wife of to-day would read it and lay its lessons to heart it would make the to-morrow much easier and happier for all of Eve's daughters."

W. G. Sperry, M. D.

"Young wives, for whom this book is intended, will receive great benefits from heeding its wise words. It is good for incitement, guidance, restraint."

Mrs. Joseph Cook

"It illuminates the Holy of Holies in the most sacred of earthly relationships with the white light of truth and purity."

Julia Holmes Smith, M. D.

"Be sure Dr. Drake's book is part of your daughter's outfit. I have never read anything which so thoroughly met the use it was designed for as this volume."

J. P. Sutherland, M. D.

"A subject difficult to treat has been handled by Dr. Drake with delicacy, earnestness and straightforwardness. It is a practical book destined to do good."

"What a Woman of Forty-five Ought to Know."

BY MRS. EMMA F. A. DRAKE, M. D.

Condensed Table of Contents

KNOWLEDGE OF CLIMACTERIC NECESSARY

Why women are not prepared to meet the climacteric—The fear that unnerves many—Error of views concerning "Change of Life"—Correct teaching stated—Influence of medical literature—Three periods in a woman's life—Relation of early habits to later aches and ills—The menopause—Conditions which influence the period of the climacteric—The age at which it usually appears—Effects of heredity—Childless women—Mothers of large families—Effects of different occupations—Excesses.

HERALDS OF CHANGE—DISEASES AND REMEDIES

Mental states during menopause—Change in blood currents—Flushes, chilliness, dizziness, etc.—Nervous symptoms—Disturbed mental and nervous equilibriums—Nature as woman's helper—Troublesome ailments—Mental troubles considered—Suggested help—Cancer—Benefits named—Apprehensions dispelled—How to banish worry—Simplifying daily duty—An eminent physician's prescription—A word to single women—Reluctance of unmarried women to meet the menopause—How to prolong one's youth—Dress during this period—The mother "At Sea"—Guarding against becoming gloomy—Effects of patent medicine advertising—Drug fiends—Lustful indulgence.

WHAT BOTH HUSBAND AND WIFE SHOULD REMEMBER

Slights and inattentions keenly felt by her—Need of patience—A word of private counsel—Value of little attentions—Wife's duty to her husband—Holding husband's affections—Making home attractive—Unselfishness.

AUTO-SUGGESTION AND OTHER SUGGESTIONS

Influence of mind over body—The mind as a curative agent—How to rise out of depression—Mental philosophy and physical betterment—Relation of health to sight—Care of the teeth—The hair—Constipation—Self cure—Choice of foods—Exercise—Physical development—Exercise of mind and soul.

Price, { $1.00 / 4 s. } net, post free.

"What a Woman of Forty-Five Ought to Know"

PRAISED BY THE PRESS

"Will dispell apprehensions aroused by groundless forebodings."—*Reformed Church Messenger.*

"If the hygienic advice in this book is followed it will lengthen the lives of women and make their closing years the happiest and most useful of all."—*Herald and Presbyter.*

"In no line of literature, perhaps, is such a book so much needed."—*New Haven Leader.*

"Those who peruse the book only from prurient curiosity will be disappointed."—*Cleveland World.*

"Should be read by every woman nearing and passing middle life."—*Pittsburg Gazette.*

"Written in that wholesome sympathetic manner characteristic of all the books in the Self and Sex Series."—*Cleveland Daily World.*

"Full of most admirable practical advice and it is written in a sympathetic manner which is the outcome of oneness of sex between the author and those whom she addresses."—*Syracuse Herald.*

"There are some things that a woman of forty-five does not know—things which she regards with more or less terror in the expectation—which terror it is the object of Mrs. Drake to dispel."—*Rochester Herald.*

"There is nothing in the book that could not be proclaimed from the house-tops, and there is everything in it that intelligent and thoughtful women should read and keep for their daughters to read when the proper time comes.—*Newark Daily Advertiser.*

NEW BOOK
......BY......
MRS. EMMA F. A. DRAKE, M.D.

"MATERNITY WITHOUT SUFFERING"

A Book for Prospective Mothers
By MRS. EMMA F. A. DRAKE, M.D.

Author of "What a Young Wife Ought to Know," and "What A Woman of 45 Ought to Know."

A valuable book for wives. A splendid and invaluable book written by a mother for mothers and prospective mothers.

It treats in a most informing and chaste manner the topics of vital interest to every mature woman.

This book, whilst having the dignity of a medical work, is couched in language that is familiar and adequate, and will prove of excellent worth to expectant mothers, as it robs this critical period of all anticipated suffering. The price of this book of priceless value to woman is only

50 Cents.   **Post Free.**   **2 Shillings.**

Table of contents sent free upon application.

The Vir Publishing Company.
(For Address see First Advertising Page.)

JUST PUBLISHED

A New Devotional Book

"Faces Toward the Light"

BY

SYLVANUS STALL, D.D.

Author of "Methods of Church Work," "Five-Minute Object Sermons to Children," "Talks to the King's Children," "Bible Selections for Daily Devotion," etc.

SOME CHAPTERS IN THE BOOK

Glory After Gloom.—The Dangerous Hour.—The Concealed Future.—Gleaning for Christ.—Hunger and Health.—Direction and Destiny.—God of the Valleys.—Coins and Christians.—Reserved Blessings.—Comfort in Sorrow.—The Better Service.—Not Knowing Whither.—Good, but Good for Nothing.—No Easy Place.—The Dead Prayer Office.—How God Reveals Himself.—Starting Late.—Source of Power.—Toiling at a Heavy Tow.—What He Gave and What He Got.—Vacation Lessons.—Wheat or Weeds, etc., etc., etc.

Price, $\left\{ \begin{array}{c} \$1.00 \\ 4\ s. \end{array} \right\}$ net, per Copy

JUST PUBLISHED

New Revised Edition

"Manhood's Morning"
BY JOSEPH ALFRED CONWELL

An Invaluable Book for Every Young Man

Chapter 1, Twelve Million Young Men. Chapter 2, The Best Years of Life. Chapter 3, What Some Young Men Have Done. Chapter 4, Wild Oats and Other Weeds. Chapter 5, Reason Why Young Men Go Wrong. Chapter 6, Paying the Piper. Chapter 7, Where Young Men Belong. Chapter 8, What Young Men Must Be. Chapter 9, What Young Men Must Do.

COMMENDATIONS

From Prof. Lyman B. Sperry, M.D., Lecturer and Author

"Every young man should read it yearly from the time he is fourteen till he is twenty-eight."

Bishop J. H. Vincent, LL.D., Chancellor of Chautauqua University

"Every minister who deals with young men, and every young man who cares to avoid evil and loves righteousness should read the book."

Frances E. Willard, President National W. C. T. U.

"We advise parents to send for a copy of this book to give as a present to their sons."

T. J. Sanders, A.M., Ph.D., President Otterbein University, Ohio

"A remarkable series of Chapters to young men—stimulating and suggestive."

Price, { $1.00 / 4 s. } net, per Copy

www.ingramcontent.com/pod-product-compliance
Lightning Source LLC
Chambersburg PA
CBHW021200230426
43667CB00006B/493